FOREWORD

The collection of "Everything Will Be Okay" travel phrasebooks published by T&P Books is designed for people traveling abroad for tourism and business. The phrasebooks contain what matters most - the essentials for basic communication. This is an indispensable set of phrases to "survive" while abroad.

This phrasebook will help you in most cases where you need to ask something, get directions, find out how much something costs, etc. It can also resolve difficult communication situations where gestures just won't help.

This book contains a lot of phrases that have been grouped according to the most relevant topics. You'll also find a mini dictionary with useful words - numbers, time, calendar, colors...

Take "Everything Will Be Okay" phrasebook with you on the road and you'll have an irreplaceable traveling companion who will help you find your way out of any situation and teach you to not fear speaking with foreigners.

TABLE OF CONTENTS

T&P Books Publishing

Travel phrasebooks collection
«Everything Will Be Okay!»

T&P Books Publishing

PHRASEBOOK

· LITHUANIAN ·

THE MOST IMPORTANT PHRASES

This phrasebook contains
the most important
phrases and questions
for basic communication
Everything you need
to survive overseas

By Andrey Taranov

T&P BOOKS

Phrasebook + 250-word dictionary

English-Lithuanian phrasebook & mini dictionary

By Andrey Taranov

The collection of "Everything Will Be Okay" travel phrasebooks published by T&P Books is designed for people traveling abroad for tourism and business. The phrasebooks contain what matters most - the essentials for basic communication. This is an indispensable set of phrases to "survive" while abroad.

You'll also find a mini dictionary with 250 useful words required for everyday communication - the names of months and days of the week, measurements, family members, and more.

T&P Books Publishing
www.tpbooks.com

ISBN: 978-1-78716-259-4

This book is also available in E-book formats.
Please visit www.tpbooks.com or the major online bookstores.

PRONUNCIATION

Letter	Lithuanian example	T&P phonetic alphabet	English example
Aa	adata	[a]	shorter than in ask
Ąą	ąžuolas	[aː]	calf, palm
Bb	badas	[b]	baby, book
Cc	cukrus	[ts]	cats, tsetse fly
Čč	česnakas	[ʧ]	church, French
Dd	dumblas	[d]	day, doctor
Ee	eglė	[æ]	chess, man
Ęę	vedęs	[æː]	longer than in brand
Ėė	ėdalas	[eː]	longer than in bell
Ff	fleita	[f]	face, food
Gg	gandras	[g]	game, gold
Hh	husaras	[ɣ]	between [g] and [h]
Ii	ižas	[i]	shorter than in feet
Įį	mįslė	[iː]	feet, meter
Yy	vynas	[iː]	feet, meter
Jj	juokas	[j]	yes, New York
Kk	kilpa	[k]	clock, kiss
Ll	laisvė	[l]	lace, people
Mm	mama	[m]	magic, milk
Nn	nauda	[n]	name, normal
Oo	ola	[o], [oː]	floor, doctor
Pp	pirtis	[p]	pencil, private
Rr	ragana	[r]	rice, radio
Ss	sostinė	[s]	city, boss
Šš	šūvis	[ʃ]	machine, shark
Tt	tėvynė	[t]	tourist, trip
Uu	upė	[u]	book
Ųų	siųsti	[uː]	pool, room
Ūū	ūmėdė	[uː]	pool, room
Vv	vabalas	[ʋ]	vase, winter
Zz	zuikis	[z]	zebra, please
Žž	žiurkė	[ʒ]	forge, pleasure

Comments

- A macron (ū), an ogonek (ą, ę, į, ų) can all be used to mark vowel length in Modern Standard Lithuanian. Acute (Áá Ą́ą́), grave (Àà), and tilde (Ãã Ą̃ą̃) diacritics are used to indicate pitch accents. However, these pitch accents are generally not written, except in dictionaries, grammars, and where needed for clarity, such as to differentiate homonyms and dialectal use.

LIST OF ABBREVIATIONS

English abbreviations

ab.	-	about
adj	-	adjective
adv	-	adverb
anim.	-	animate
as adj	-	attributive noun used as adjective
e.g.	-	for example
etc.	-	et cetera
fam.	-	familiar
fem.	-	feminine
form.	-	formal
inanim.	-	inanimate
masc.	-	masculine
math	-	mathematics
mil.	-	military
n	-	noun
pl	-	plural
pron.	-	pronoun
sb	-	somebody
sing.	-	singular
sth	-	something
v aux	-	auxiliary verb
vi	-	intransitive verb
vi, vt	-	intransitive, transitive verb
vt	-	transitive verb

Lithuanian abbreviations

dgs	-	plural
m	-	feminine noun
m dgs	-	feminine plural
v	-	masculine noun
v dgs	-	masculine plural

T&P BOOKS

LITHUANIAN PHRASEBOOK

This section contains important phrases that may come in handy in various real-life situations.
The phrasebook will help you ask for directions, clarify a price, buy tickets, and order food at a restaurant

T&P Books Publishing

PHRASEBOOK
CONTENTS

T&P Books Publishing

Excuse me, ...	**Atsiprašaū, ...** [atsʲɪpra'ʃɑʊ, ...]
Hello.	**Sveikì.** [svʲɛɪ'kʲɪ.]
Thank you.	**Áčiū.** ['a:tʂʲu:.]
Good bye.	**Ikì.** [ɪ'kʲɪ.]
Yes.	**Taìp.** ['tʌɪp.]
No.	**Nè.** ['nʲɛ.]
I don't know.	**Nežinaū.** [nʲɛʒʲɪ'nɑʊ.]
Where? | Where to? | When?	**Kur̃? | Kur? | Kadà?** ['kʊr? | 'kʊr? | ka'da?]
I need ...	**Mán reĩkia ...** ['man 'rʲɛɪkʲɛ ...]
I want ...	**Nóriu ...** ['norʲʊ ...]
Do you have ...?	**Ar̃ tùrite ...?** [ar 'tʊrʲɪtʲɛ ...?]
Is there a ... here?	**Ar̃ čià yrà ...?** [ar 'tʂʲæ i:'ra ...?]
May I ...?	**Ar̃ galiù ...?** [ar ga'lʲʊ ...?]
..., please (polite request)	**Prašaū ...** [pra'ʃɑʊ ...]
I'm looking for ...	**Ieškau ...** ['ɪʲɛʃkɑʊ ...]
restroom	**tualèto** [tʊa'lʲɛtɔ]
ATM	**bankomãto** [baŋko'ma:tɔ]
pharmacy (drugstore)	**váistinės** ['vʌɪstʲɪnʲeːs]
hospital	**ligóninės** [lʲɪ'gonʲɪnʲeːs]
police station	**polìcijos skỹriaus** [po'lʲɪtsɪjɔs 'skʲiːrʲɛʊs]
subway	**metrò** [mʲɛ'tro]

taxi	**taksì** [tak'sʲɪ]
train station	**traukinių stotiễs** [trɑʊkʲɪ'nʲuː sto'tʲɛs]

My name is ...	**Mãno vardas ...** ['maːnɔ 'vardas ...]
What's your name?	**Kuõ jŭs vardù?** ['kʊɑ 'juːs var'dʊ?]
Could you please help me?	**Atsiprašaũ, ar gãlite padéti?** [atsʲɪpra'ʃɑʊ, ar 'gaːlʲɪte pa'dʲeːtʲɪ?]
I've got a problem.	**Atsitìko problemà.** [atsʲɪ'tʲɪkɔ problʲɛ'ma.]
I don't feel well.	**Mán blogà.** ['man blʲo'ga.]
Call an ambulance!	**Kvieskite greitają!** ['kvʲɛskʲɪtʲɛ 'grʲɛɪtaːja:!]
May I make a call?	**Ar galiù paskambinti?** [ar ga'lʲʊ pas'kambʲɪntʲɪ?]

I'm sorry.	**Atsiprašaũ.** [atsʲɪpra'ʃɑʊ.]
You're welcome.	**Nerà ùž ką.** [nʲe:'ra 'ʊʒ ka:.]

I, me	**àš** ['aʃ]
you (inform.)	**tù** ['tʊ]
he	**jìs** [jɪs]
she	**jì** [jɪ]
they (masc.)	**jiẽ** ['jiɛ]
they (fem.)	**jõs** ['jɔːs]
we	**mẽs** ['mʲæs]
you (pl)	**jŭs** ['juːs]
you (sg, form.)	**Jŭs** ['juːs]

ENTRANCE	**ĮĖJÌMAS** [iːʲɛːˈjɪmas]
EXIT	**IŠĖJÌMAS** [ɪʃeːˈjɪmas]
OUT OF ORDER	**NEVEĨKIA** [nʲɛ'vʲɛɪkʲɛ]
CLOSED	**UŽDARÝTA** [ʊʒda'rʲiːta]

OPEN	**ATIDARYTA** [atˈɪdaˈrʲiːta]
FOR WOMEN	**MÓTERŲ** [ˈmotʲɛruː]
FOR MEN	**VÝRŲ** [ˈvʲiːruː]

Questions

Where?	**Kur̃?** ['kʊr?]
Where to?	**Į kur̃?** [i: 'kʊr?]
Where from?	**Iš kur̃?** [ɪʃ 'kʊr?]
Why?	**Kodėl?** [kɔ'dʲeːlʲ?]
For what reason?	**Kodėl?** [kɔ'dʲeːlʲ?]
When?	**Kadà?** [ka'da?]
How long?	**Kíek laĩko?** ['kʲiɛk 'lʲʌɪko?]
At what time?	**Kadà?** [ka'da?]
How much?	**Kíek?** ['kʲiɛk?]
Do you have ...?	**Ar̃ tùrite ...?** [ar 'tʊrʲɪtʲɛ ...?]
Where is ...?	**Kur̃ yrà ...?** ['kʊr iː'ra ...?]
What time is it?	**Kíek dabar̃ valandų̃?** ['kʲiɛk da'bar valʲan'du:?]
May I make a call?	**Ar̃ galiù paskam̃binti?** [ar ga'lʲʊ pas'kambʲɪntʲɪ?]
Who's there?	**Kàs teñ?** ['kas tʲɛn?]
Can I smoke here?	**Ar̃ čià galimà rūkýti?** [ar 'tʂʲæ galʲɪ'ma ruː'kʲiːtʲɪ?]
May I ...?	**Ar̃ galiù ...?** [ar ga'lʲʊ ...?]

Needs

I'd like ...	**Norečiau ...** [no'r'e:tʂ'ɛʊ ...]
I don't want ...	**Nenoriu ...** [n'ɛ'nor'ʊ ...]
I'm thirsty.	**Noriu atsigérti.** ['nor'ʊ ats'ɪ'g'ɛrt'ɪ.]
I want to sleep.	**Noriu miégo.** ['nor'ʊ 'm'ɛgɔ.]
I want ...	**Noriu ...** ['nor'ʊ ...]
to wash up	**nusipraũsti** [nʊs'ɪ'praʊst'ɪ]
to brush my teeth	**išsivalýti dantìs** [ɪʃs'iva'l'i:t'ɪ dan't'ɪs]
to rest a while	**trupùtį pailséti** [trʊ'pʊt'ɪː pʌɪl'ʲs'e:t'ɪ]
to change my clothes	**pérsirengti** ['p'ɛrs'ɪr'ɛŋkt'ɪ]
to go back to the hotel	**grį̃žti i viešbutį** ['gr'i:ʒt'ɪ ɪ 'v'ɛʃbʊt'i:]
to buy ...	**nusipírkti ...** [nʊs'ɪ'p'ɪrkt'ɪ ...]
to go to ...	**eĩti į̃ ...** ['ɛɪt'ɪ i: ...]
to visit ...	**aplankýti ...** [ap'ʲaŋ'k'i:t'ɪ ...]
to meet with ...	**susitìkti sù ...** [sʊs'ɪ't'ɪkt'ɪ 'sʊ ...]
to make a call	**paskambinti** [pas'kamb'ɪnt'ɪ]
I'm tired.	**Àš pavar̃gęs /pavar̃gusi/.** ['aʃ pa'varg'ɛːs /pa'vargʊs'ɪ/.]
We are tired.	**Mẽs pavar̃gome.** ['m'æs pa'vargom'ɛ.]
I'm cold.	**Mán šálta.** ['man 'ʃal'ta.]
I'm hot.	**Mán karštà.** ['man karʃta.]
I'm OK.	**Mán vìskas geraĩ.** ['man 'v'ɪskas g'ɛ'rʌɪ.]

I need to make a call.

Mán reĭkia paskaṁbinti.
['man 'rɛɪkʲɛ pasˈkambʲɪntʲɪ.]

I need to go to the restroom.

Mán reĭkia į̇̃ tualėtą.
['man rʲɛɪkʲɛ iː tʊaˈlʲɛtaː.]

I have to go.

Mán reĭkia eĭti.
['man 'rʲɛɪkʲɛ 'ɛɪtʲɪ.]

I have to go now.

Mán jaū reĭkia eĭti.
['man jɛʊ 'rʲɛɪkʲɛ 'ɛɪtʲɪ.]

Asking for directions

Excuse me, ...	**Atsiprašaũ, ...** [atsʲɪpra'ʃɑʋ, ...]
Where is ...?	**Kuř yrà ...?** ['kʊr iː'ra ...?]
Which way is ...?	**Į̃ kurią̃ pùsę yrà ...?** [i: kʊ'rʲæ: 'pʊsʲɛː iː'ra ...?]
Could you help me, please?	**Atsiprašaũ, ař gãlite padéti?** [atsʲɪpra'ʃɑʋ, ar 'gaːlʲɪte pa'dʲeːtʲɪ?]
I'm looking for ...	**Àš íeškau ...** ['aʃ 'ʲɛʃkɑʋ ...]
I'm looking for the exit.	**Àš íeškau išėjìmo.** ['aʃ 'ʲɛʃkɑʋ iʃʲeː'jɪmɔ.]
I'm going to ...	**Àš einù į̃ ...** ['aʃ ɛɪ'nʋ iː ...]
Am I going the right way to ...?	**Ař àš teisìngai einù į̃ ...?** [ar 'aʃ tʲɛɪ'sʲɪːngʌɪ ɛɪ'nʋ iː ...?]
Is it far?	**Ař tolì?** [ar to'lʲɪ?]
Can I get there on foot?	**Ař galiù nueĩti teñ pésčiomìs?** [ar ga'lʲʋ 'nʋɛɪtʲɪ ten pʲeːstʃʲo'mʲɪs?]
Can you show me on the map?	**Ař gãlite paródyti žemélapyje?** [ar 'gaːlʲɪte pa'rodʲiːtʲɪ ʒe'mʲeːlapʲiːje?]
Show me where we are right now.	**Paródykite, kuř dabař ẽsame.** [pa'rodʲiːkʲɪtʲɛ, kʊr da'bar 'ɛsamʲɛ.]
Here	**Čià** ['tʂʲæ]
There	**Teñ** ['tʲɛn]
This way	**Eimè čià** [ɛɪ'mʲɛ tʂʲæ]
Turn right.	**Sùkite dešinẽn.** ['sʊkʲɪte deʃɪ'nʲeːn.]
Turn left.	**Sùkite kairẽn.** ['sʊkʲɪte kʌɪ'rʲeːn.]
first (second, third) turn	**pìrmas (añtras, trẽčias) pósūkis** ['pʲɪrmas ('antras, 'trʲeːtʃiɛs) 'posuːkʲɪs]

to the right

į dešinę
[i: 'dʲæʃɪnʲɛ:]

to the left

į kairę
[i: 'kʌɪrʲɛ:]

Go straight ahead.

Eikite tiesiai.
['ɛɪkʲɪtʲɛ 'tʲɛsʲɛɪ.]

Signs

WELCOME!	**SVEIKÌ ATVŸKĘ!** [svʲɛɪ'kʲɪ at'vʲi:kʲɛ:ļ]
ENTRANCE	**ĮĖJÌMAS** [i:ʲɛ:'jɪmas]
EXIT	**IŠĖJÌMAS** [ɪʃʲe:'jɪmas]
PUSH	**STÙMTI** ['stʊmtʲɪ]
PULL	**TRAÚKTI** ['trɑʊktʲɪ]
OPEN	**ATIDARÝTA** [atʲɪda'rʲi:ta]
CLOSED	**UŽDARÝTA** [ʊʒda'rʲi:ta]
FOR WOMEN	**MÓTERŲ** ['motʲɛru:]
FOR MEN	**VÝRŲ** ['vʲi:ru:]
GENTLEMEN, GENTS (m)	**VÝRŲ** ['vʲi:ru:]
WOMEN (f)	**MÓTERŲ** ['motʲɛru:]
DISCOUNTS	**NUÓLAIDOS** ['nʊolʲʌɪdos]
SALE	**IŠPARDAVÌMAS** [ɪʃparda'vʲɪmas]
FREE	**NEMÓKAMAI** [nʲɛ'mokamʌɪ]
NEW!	**NAUJÍENA!** [nɑʊ'jiɛna!]
ATTENTION!	**DĖMESIO!** ['dʲe:mesʲoļ]
NO VACANCIES	**LAISVŲ VIÈTŲ NĖRÀ** [lʲʌɪs'vu: 'vʲɛtu: nʲe:'ra]
RESERVED	**REZERVUÓTA** [rʲɛzʲɛr'vʊota]
ADMINISTRATION	**ADMINISTRÃCIJA** [admʲɪnʲɪs'tra:tsʲɪja]
STAFF ONLY	**TÌK PERSONÁLUI** ['tʲɪk pʲɛrso'nalʲʊi]

BEWARE OF THE DOG!	**ATSARGIAĨ, ŠUÕ!** [atsar'gʲɛɪ, 'ʃʊɑ!]
NO SMOKING!	**NERŪKÝTI!** [nʲɛru:'kʲi:tʲɪ!]
DO NOT TOUCH!	**NELIÉSTI!** [nʲɛ'lʲɛstʲɪ!]
DANGEROUS	**PAVOJÌNGA** [pavo'jɪnga]
DANGER	**PAVÕJUS** [pa'vo:jʊs]
HIGH VOLTAGE	**AUKŠTÀ ĮTAMPA** [ɑʊkʃta 'i:tampa]
NO SWIMMING!	**NESIMÁUDYTI!** [nʲɛsʲɪ'mɑʊdʲi:tʲɪ!]
OUT OF ORDER	**NEVEĨKIA** [nʲɛ'vʲɛɪkʲæ]
FLAMMABLE	**DEGÙ** [dʲɛ'gʊ]
FORBIDDEN	**UŽDRAUSTÀ** [ʊʒdrɑʊs'ta]
NO TRESPASSING!	**PRAĖJÌMO NĖRÀ!** [praʲe:'jɪmɔ nʲe:'ra!]
WET PAINT	**DAŽÝTA** [da'ʒʲi:ta]
CLOSED FOR RENOVATIONS	**UŽDARÝTA REMÒNTUI** [ʊʒda'rʲi:ta rʲɛ'montʊi]
WORKS AHEAD	**KĖLIO DARBAĨ** ['kʲælʲɔ dar'bʌɪ]
DETOUR	**APÝLANKA** [a'pʲi:lʲaŋka]

Transportation. General phrases

plane	**lėktùvas** [lʲeːkˈtʊvas]
train	**traukinỹs** [traʊkʲɪˈnʲiːs]
bus	**autobùsas** [aʊtoˈbʊsas]
ferry	**kéltas** [ˈkʲɛlʲtas]
taxi	**taksì** [takˈsʲɪ]
car	**automobìlis** [aʊtomoˈbʲɪlʲɪs]
schedule	**tvarkãraštis** [tvarˈkaːraʃtʲɪs]
Where can I see the schedule?	**Kur galiù ràsti tvarkãraštį?** [ˈkʊr gaˈlʲʊ ˈrastʲɪ tvarˈkaːraʃtʲɪ:?]
workdays (weekdays)	**dárbo dienomìs** [ˈdarbɔ dʲiɛnoˈmʲɪs]
weekends	**savàitgaliais** [saˈvʌɪtgalʲɛɪs]
holidays	**šveñtinėmis dienomìs** [ˈʃvʲentʲɪnʲeːmʲɪs dʲiɛnoˈmʲɪs]
DEPARTURE	**IŠVYKÌMAS** [ɪʃvʲiːˈkʲɪmas]
ARRIVAL	**ATVYKÌMAS** [atvʲiːˈkʲɪmas]
DELAYED	**ATIDĖ́TAS** [atʲɪˈdʲeːtas]
CANCELLED	**ÀTŠAUKTAS** [ˈatʃaʊktas]
next (train, etc.)	**kìtas** [ˈkʲɪtas]
first	**pìrmas** [ˈpʲɪrmas]
last	**paskutìnis** [paskʊˈtʲɪnʲɪs]
When is the next ...?	**Kadà kìtas ...?** [kaˈda ˈkʲɪtas ...?]
When is the first ...?	**Kadà pìrmas ...?** [kaˈda ˈpʲɪrmas ...?]

When is the last ...?

Kadà paskutìnis ...?
[ka'da pasku't'ɪnʲɪs ...?]

transfer (change of trains, etc.)

pérsėdimas
['pʲɛrsʲe:dʲɪmas]

to make a transfer

pérsėsti
['pʲɛrsʲe:stʲɪ]

Do I need to make a transfer?

Ar̃ mán reĩkia pérsėsti?
[ar 'man 'rʲɛɪkʲɛ 'pʲærsʲe:stʲɪ?]

Buying tickets

Where can I buy tickets?	**Kur galiù nusipírkti bìlietą?** ['kʊr ga'lʲʊ nʊsʲɪ'pʲɪrktʲɪ 'bʲɪlʲiɛta:?]
ticket	**bìlietas** ['bʲɪlʲiɛtas]
to buy a ticket	**nusipírkti bìlietą** [nʊsʲɪ'pʲɪrktʲɪ 'bʲɪlʲiɛta:]
ticket price	**bìlieto káina** ['bʲɪlʲiɛtɔ 'kʌɪna]
Where to?	**Į̃ kur̃?** [i: 'kʊr?]
To what station?	**Į̃ kurią̃ stótį?** [i: kʊ'rʲæ: 'stoːtʲɪ:?]
I need ...	**Mán reĩkia ...** ['man 'rʲɛɪkʲɛ ...]
one ticket	**víeno bìlieto** ['vʲiɛnɔ 'bʲɪlʲiɛtɔ]
two tickets	**dviejų̃ bìlietų** [dvʲiɛ'ju: 'bʲɪlʲiɛtu:]
three tickets	**trijų̃ bìlietų** [trʲɪ'ju: 'bʲɪlʲiɛtu:]
one-way	**į̃ víeną pùsę** [i: 'vʲiɛna: 'pʊsʲɛ:]
round-trip	**pirmỹn - atgal̃** [pʲɪr'mʲiːn - at'galʲ]
first class	**pirmą́ja klasė̃** [pʲɪr'maːja klʲa'sʲɛ]
second class	**antrą́ja klasė̃** [ant'raːja klʲa'sʲɛ]
tóday	**šiañdien** ['ʃændʲiɛn]
tomorrow	**rytój** [rʲiː'toj]
the day after tomorrow	**porýt** [po'rʲiːt]
in the morning	**rytė̃** [rʲiː'tʲɛ]
in the afternoon	**põ pietų̃** ['po: pʲiɛ'tu:]
in the evening	**vakarė̃** [vaka'rʲɛ]

aisle seat	**vietà priẽ praėjìmo** [vʲiɛ'ta prʲɛ praʲe:'jɪmɔ]
window seat	**vietà priẽ lángo** [vʲiɛ'ta prʲɛ 'lʲangɔ]
How much?	**Kíek?** ['kʲiɛk?]
Can I pay by credit card?	**Aȓ galiù mokéti kredìto kortelė̃?** [ar ga'lʲʊ mo'kʲe:tʲɪ kre'dʲɪtɔ korte'lʲɛ?]

Bus

bus	**autobùsas** [auto'busas]
intercity bus	**tarpmiestìnis autobùsas** [tarpmʲiɛs'tʲɪnʲɪs auto'busas]
bus stop	**autobùsų stotėlė** [auto'busu: sto'tʲælʲe:]
Where's the nearest bus stop?	**Kur̃ yrà arčiáusia autobùsų stotėlė?** ['kur i:'ra ar'tʂʲæusʲɛ auto'busu: sto'tʲælʲe:?]
number (bus ~, etc.)	**nùmeris** ['numʲɛrʲɪs]
Which bus do I take to get to ...?	**Kuriuõ autobusų galimà nuvažiuoti į ...?** [ku'rʲuo: autobu'su galʲɪ'ma nuva'ʐʲuotʲɪ i: ...?]
Does this bus go to ...?	**Ar̃ šìs autobùsas važiúoja į ...?** [ar ʃɪ:s auto'busas va'ʐʲuo:jɛ i: ...?]
How frequent are the buses?	**Kàs kíek laĩko važiúoja autobùsai?** ['kas 'kʲiɛk 'lʲʌɪkɔ va'ʐʲuɑ:jɛ auto'busʌɪ?]
every 15 minutes	**kàs penkiólika minùčių** ['kas pʲɛnʲ'kʲolʲɪka mʲɪ'nutʂʲu:]
every half hour	**kàs pùsvalandį** ['kas 'pusvalʲandʲɪ:]
every hour	**kàs vãlandą** ['kas 'va:lʲanda:]
several times a day	**Kelìs kartùs per̃ dièną** [kʲɛ'lʲɪs kar'tus pʲɛr 'dʲɛna:]
... times a day	**... kartùs per̃ dièną** [... kar'tus pʲɛr 'dʲɛna:]
schedule	**tvarkãraštis** [tvar'ka:raʃtʲɪs]
Where can I see the schedule?	**Kur̃ galiù ràsti tvarkãraštį?** ['kur ga'lʲu 'rastʲɪ tvar'ka:raʃtʲɪ:?]
When is the next bus?	**Kadà kìtas autobùsas?** [ka'da 'kʲɪtas auto'busas?]
When is the first bus?	**Kadà pìrmas autobùsas?** [ka'da 'pʲɪrmas auto'busas?]
When is the last bus?	**Kadà paskutìnis autobùsas?** [ka'da pasku'tʲɪnʲɪs auto'busas?]

stop

stotelė
[sto'tʲælʲe:]

next stop

kità stotelė
[kʲɪ'ta sto'tʲælʲe:]

last stop (terminus)

paskutinė maršrùto stotelė
[pasku'tʲɪnʲe: marʃrʊtɔ sto'tʲælʲe:]

Stop here, please.

Prašaũ, sustókite čià.
[pra'ʃɑʊ, sʊs'tokʲɪtʲɛ tʂʲæ.]

Excuse me, this is my stop.

Atsiprašaũ, taĩ māno stotelė.
[atsʲɪpra'ʃɑʊ, tʌɪ 'ma:nɔ sto'tʲælʲe:.]

Train

train	**traukinỹs** [trɑʊkʲɪˈnʲiːs]
suburban train	**priemiestìnis traukinỹs** [prʲiɛmʲiɛsˈtʲɪnʲɪs trɑʊkʲɪˈnʲiːs]
long-distance train	**tarpmiestìnis traukinỹs** [tarpmʲiɛsˈtʲɪnʲɪs trɑʊkʲɪˈnʲiːs]
train station	**traukinių̃ stotìs** [trɑʊkʲɪˈnʲu: stoˈtʲɪs]
Excuse me, where is the exit to the platform?	**Atsiprašaũ, kur̃ yrà išėjimas į̃ peroną?** [atsʲɪpraˈʃɑʊ, kʊr iːˈra iʃʲeːˈjɪmas iː peˈrona:?]

Does this train go to ...?	**Ar̃ šìs traukinỹs važiúoja į̃ ...?** [ar ʃɪːs trɑʊkʲɪˈnʲiːs vaˈʒʲʊoːjɛ iː ...?]
next train	**kìtas traukinỹs** ['kʲɪtas trɑʊkʲɪˈnʲiːs]
When is the next train?	**Kadà kìtas traukinỹs?** [kaˈda kʲɪtas trɑʊkʲɪˈnʲiːs?]
Where can I see the schedule?	**Kur̃ galiù ràsti tvarkãraštį?** ['kʊr gaˈlʲʊ 'rastʲɪ tvar'ka:raʃtʲɪ:?]
From which platform?	**Ìš kuriõ perono?** [ɪʃ kʊˈrʲoː pʲɛˈrono?]
When does the train arrive in ...?	**Kadà traukinỹs atvažiúos į̃ ...?** [kaˈda trɑʊkʲɪˈnʲɪːs atvaˈʒʲʊoːs iː ...?]

Please help me.	**Prašaũ, padékite mán.** [praˈʃɑʊ, paˈdʲeːkʲɪte 'man.]
I'm looking for my seat.	**Ìeškau sàvo viẽtos.** ['ɪʲɛʃkɑʊ 'savɔ 'vʲɛtos.]
We're looking for our seats.	**Ìeškome sàvo viẽtų.** ['ɪʲɛʃkomʲɛ 'savɔ 'vʲɛtu:.]
My seat is taken.	**Màno vietà užimtà.** ['manɔ vʲiɛˈta ʊʒʲɪmˈta.]
Our seats are taken.	**Mū́sų viẽtos ùžimtos.** ['mu:su: 'vʲɛtos 'ʊʒʲɪmtos.]

I'm sorry but this is my seat.	**Atsiprašaũ, bèt taĩ màno vietà.** [atsʲɪpraˈʃɑʊ, bʲɛt tʌɪ 'ma:nɔ vʲiɛ'ta.]
Is this seat taken?	**Ar̃ šì vietà užimtà?** [ar ʃɪ vʲiɛ'ta ʊʒʲɪm'ta?]
May I sit here?	**Ar̃ galiù čià atsisésti?** [ar gaˈlʲʊ 'tʂʲæ atsʲɪˈsʲeːstʲɪ?]

On the train. Dialogue (No ticket)

Ticket, please.

Prašaū paródyti bìlietą.
[praˈʃɒʊ paˈrodʲiːtʲɪ bʲɪlʲiɛtaː.]

I don't have a ticket.

Àš neturiù bìlieto.
[ˈaʃ nʲɛtuˈrʲʊ ˈbʲɪlʲiɛtɔ.]

I lost my ticket.

Pàmečiau sàvo bìlietą.
[ˈpamʲɛtʂɛʊ ˈsavɔ ˈbʲɪlʲiɛtaː.]

I forgot my ticket at home.

Pamiršaū sàvo bìlietą namuosė.
[pamʲɪrˈʃɒʊ ˈsavɔ ˈbʲɪlʲiɛtaː namʊɒˈsʲɛ.]

You can buy a ticket from me.

Gãlite nusipìrkti bìlietą ìš manęs.
[ˈɡaːlʲɪtʲɛ nʊsʲɪˈpʲɪrktʲɪ ˈbʲɪlʲiɛta: ɪʃ maˈnʲɛ:s.]

You will also have to pay a fine.

Taïp pàt turėsite sumokéti baūdą.
[ˈtʌɪp ˈpat tʊˈrʲeːsʲɪtɛ sʊmoˈkʲeːtʲɪ ˈbɒʊda:.]

Okay.

Geraĩ.
[ɡʲɛˈrʌɪ.]

Where are you going?

Kuř važiúojate?
[ˈkʊr vaˈʒʲʊoːjɛtʲɛ?]

I'm going to …

Važiúoju į̇̃ …
[vaˈʒʲʊoːjʊ iː …]

How much? I don't understand.

Kíek? Àš nesuprantù.
[ˈkʲiɛk? aʃ nʲɛsʊpranˈtʊ.]

Write it down, please.

Ař gãlite užrašýti?
[ar ˈɡaːlʲɪtʲɛ ʊʒraˈʃiːtʲɪ?]

Okay. Can I pay with a credit card?

Geraĩ. Ař galiù mokéti kredìto kortele?
[ɡʲɛˈrʌɪ. ar ɡaˈlʲʊ moˈkʲeːtʲɪ kreˈdʲɪtɔ korteˈlʲɛ?]

Yes, you can.

Taïp, gãlite.
[ˈtʌɪp, ˈɡaːlʲɪtʲɛ.]

Here's your receipt.

Štaĩ jū́sų čèkis.
[ˈʃtʌɪ ˈjuːsu: ˈtʂʲɛkʲɪs.]

Sorry about the fine.

Atsiprašaū dė̃l baudõs.
[atsʲɪpraˈʃɒʊ dʲeːlʲ bɒʊˈdoːs.]

That's okay. It was my fault.

Niẽko, taĩ māno kaltė̃.
[ˈnʲɛko, ˈtʌɪ ˈma:nɔ kalʲtʲeː.]

Enjoy your trip.

Gẽros keliõnės.
[ˈɡʲɛro:s kʲɛˈlʲionʲɛs.]

Taxi

taxi	**taksì** [tak'sʲɪ]
taxi driver	**taksì vairúotojas** [tak'sʲɪ vʌɪ'rʊoto:jɛs]
to catch a taxi	**susistabdýti taksì** [sʊsʲɪstab'dʲi:tʲɪ tak'sʲɪ]
taxi stand	**taksì stotėlė** [tak'sʲɪ sto'tʲælʲe:]
Where can I get a taxi?	**Kur̃ galiù išsikviẽsti taksì?** ['kʊr ga'lʲʊ ɪʃsʲɪk'vʲɛstʲɪ tak'sʲɪ?]
to call a taxi	**išsikviẽsti taksì** [ɪʃsʲɪ'kvʲɛstʲɪ tak'sʲɪ]
I need a taxi.	**Mán reĩkia taksì.** ['man 'rʲɛɪkʲɛ tak'sʲɪ.]
Right now.	**Dabar̃.** [da'bar.]
What is your address (location)?	**Kóks jū́sų ãdresas?** ['koks 'ju:su: 'a:drʲɛsas?]
My address is ...	**Màno ãdresas yrà...** ['manɔ 'a:drʲɛsas i:'ra...]
Your destination?	**Kur̃ važiúosite?** ['kʊr va'ʒʲʊosʲɪtʲɛ?]
Excuse me, ...	**Atsiprašaũ, ...** [atsʲɪpra'ʃɑʊ, ...]
Are you available?	**Ar̃ Jū̃s neùžimtas?** [ar 'ju:s 'nʲɛʊ ʒʲɪmtas?]
How much is it to get to ...?	**Kíek kainúotų nuvažiúoti į̃ ...?** ['kʲiɛk kʌɪ'nʊotu: nʊva'ʒʲʊotʲɪ i: ...?]
Do you know where it is?	**Ar̃ žìnote, kur̃ taĩ yrà?** [ar 'ʒʲɪnotʲɛ, kʊr tʌɪ i:'ra?]
Airport, please.	**Į̃ óro úostą.** [i: 'orɔ 'ʊasta:.]
Stop here, please.	**Sustókite čià, prašaũ.** [sʊs'tokʲɪtʲɛ tʂʲæ, pra'ʃɑʊ.]
It's not here.	**Taĩ nè čià.** ['tʌɪ nʲɛ 'tʂʲæ.]
This is the wrong address.	**Čià nè tàs ãdresas.** ['tʂʲæ nʲɛ 'tas 'a:drʲɛsas.]
Turn left.	**Sùkite kairẽn.** ['sʊkʲɪtʲɛ kʌɪ'rʲe:n.]
Turn right.	**Sùkite dešinẽn.** ['sʊkʲɪtʲɛ deʃʲɪ'nʲe:n.]

How much do I owe you?

Kíek àš skolìngas/skolìnga?
['kʲiɛk aʃ sko'lʲɪngas /sko'lʲɪnga?/]

I'd like a receipt, please.

Noréčiau čekio.
[no'rʲe:tsʲɛʊ 'tsʲɛkʲɔ.]

Keep the change.

Grą̃žą pasilìkite.
[gra:'ʒa: pasʲɪ'lʲɪkʲɪtʲɛ.]

Would you please wait for me?

Prašaũ mãnęs paláukti.
[pra'ʃɑʊ 'ma:nʲɛ:s pa'lʲɑʊktʲɪ.]

five minutes

penkiàs minutès
[pʲɛŋ'kʲæs mʲɪnʊ'tʲɛs]

ten minutes

dẽšimt minùčių
['dʲæʃɪmt mʲɪ'nʊtsʲu:]

fifteen minutes

penkiólika minùčių
[pʲɛŋ'kʲolʲɪka mʲɪ'nʊtsʲu:]

twenty minutes

dvìdešimt minùčių
['dvʲɪdʲɛʃɪmt mʲɪ'nʊtsʲu:]

half an hour

pùsvalandį
['pʊsvalʲandʲɪ:]

Hotel

Hello.	**Sveiki.** [svʲɛɪˈkʲɪ.]
My name is …	**Māno vardas …** [ˈmaːnɔ ˈvardas …]
I have a reservation.	**Aš rezervavau kambarį.** [ˈaʃ rʲɛzʲɛrvaˈvɑʊ ˈkambarʲɪː.]
I need …	**Man reikia …** [ˈman ˈrʲɛɪkʲɛ …]
a single room	**kambario vienam žmogui** [ˈkambarʲɔ vʲɛˈnam ˈʒmogui]
a double room	**kambario dviems žmonėms** [ˈkambarʲɔ ˈdvʲiɛms ʒmoˈnʲeːms]
How much is that?	**Kiek tai kainuos?** [ˈkʲiɛk ˈtɑɪ kʌɪˈnuɑs?]
That's a bit expensive.	**Truputį brangu.** [trʊˈpʊti: branˈgʊ.]
Do you have anything else?	**Ar turite kažką kito?** [ar ˈtʊrʲɪtʲɛ kaʒˈka: ˈkʲɪto?]
I'll take it.	**Paimsiu.** [ˈpʌɪmsʲʊ.]
I'll pay in cash.	**Mokėsiu grynais.** [moˈkʲeːsʲʊ grʲɪːˈnʌɪs.]
I've got a problem.	**Turiu problemą.** [tʊˈrʲʊ probˈlʲɛma:.]
My … is broken.	**Sulūžo mano … .** [sʊˈlʲuːʒɔ ˈmanɔ …]
My … is out of order.	**Neveikia mano … .** [nʲɛˈvʲɛɪkʲɛ ˈmanɔ …]
TV	**televizorius** [tʲɛlʲɛˈvʲɪzorʲʊs]
air conditioner	**oro kondicionierius** [ˈorɔ kondʲɪtsʲɪjɔˈnʲɛrʲʊs]
tap	**čiaupas** [ˈtʃʲæʊpas]
shower	**dušas** [ˈdʊʃas]
sink	**praustuvė** [prɑʊsˈtʊvʲeː]
safe	**seifas** [ˈsʲɛɪfas]

door lock	**durų spyna** [dʊˈru: spʲiːˈna]
electrical outlet	**elektros lizdas** [ɛˈlʲɛktros ˈlʲɪzdas]
hairdryer	**plaukų džiovintuvas** [plʲɑʊˈku: dʒʲovʲɪnˈtʊvas]

I don't have …	**Aš neturiu …** [ˈaʃ nʲɛtʊˈrʲʊ …]
water	**vandens** [vanˈdʲɛns]
light	**šviesos** [ʃvʲiɛˈsoːs]
electricity	**elektros** [ɛˈlʲɛktros]

Can you give me …?	**Ar galite duoti …?** [ar ˈgaːlʲɪtʲɛ ˈdʊotʲɪ …?]
a towel	**rankšluostį** [ˈraŋkʃlʲʊɑstiː]
a blanket	**antklodę** [ˈantklʲodʲɛː]
slippers	**šlepetės** [ʃlʲɛpʲɛˈtʲɛs]
a robe	**chalatą** [xaˈlʲaːtaː]
shampoo	**šampūno** [ʃamˈpuːnɔ]
soap	**muilo** [ˈmʊɪlʲɔ]

I'd like to change rooms.	**Norėčiau pakeisti kambarį.** [noˈrʲeːtʃʲɛʊ paˈkʲɛɪstʲɪ ˈkambarʲɪː.]
I can't find my key.	**Nerandu savo rakto.** [nʲɛranˈdʊ ˈsavɔ ˈraːktɔ.]
Could you open my room, please?	**Ar galite atrakinti mano kambarį?** [ar ˈgaːlʲɪtʲɛ atrakʲɪːntʲɪ ˈmanɔ ˈkambarʲɪ?]
Who's there?	**Kas ten?** [ˈkas tʲɛn?]
Come in!	**Užeikite!** [ʊˈʒʲɛɪkʲɪtʲɛ!]
Just a minute!	**Palaukite minutę!** [paˈlʲɑʊkʲɪtʲɛ mʲɪˈnʊtʲɛː!]
Not right now, please.	**Ne dabar, prašau.** [ˈnʲɛ daˈbar, praˈʃɑʊ.]

Come to my room, please.	**Prašau, užeikite į mano kambarį.** [praˈʃɑʊ, ʊˈʒʲɛɪkʲɪtʲɛ iː ˈmanɔ ˈkambarʲɪː.]
I'd like to order food service.	**Norėčiau užsisakyti maisto.** [noˈrʲeːtʃʲɛʊ ʊʒsʲɪsaˈkʲiːtʲɪ ˈmʌɪstɔ.]
My room number is …	**Mano kambario numeris …** [ˈmaːnɔ ˈkambarʲɔ ˈnʊmʲɛrʲɪs …]

I'm leaving ...	**Àš išvykstù ...** [ˈaʃ iʃvʲiːksˈtʊ ...]
We're leaving ...	**Mḗs išvỹkstame ...** [ˈmʲæs iʃˈvʲiːkstamʲɛ ...]
right now	**dabar̃** [daˈbar]
this afternoon	**põ pietų̃** [ˈpoː pʲiɛˈtuː]
tonight	**šią̃nakt** [ˈʃæːnakt]
tomorrow	**rytój** [rʲiːˈtoj]
tomorrow morning	**rýt rytè** [ˈrʲiːt rʲiːˈtʲɛ]
tomorrow evening	**rýt vakarè** [ˈrʲiːt vakaˈrʲɛ]
the day after tomorrow	**porýt** [poˈrʲiːt]

I'd like to pay.	**Norė́čiau sumokė́ti.** [noˈrʲeːtʂʲɛʊ sumoˈkʲeːtʲɪ]
Everything was wonderful.	**Vìskas bùvo nuostabù.** [ˈvʲɪskas ˈbʊvɔ nʊɑstaˈbʊ]
Where can I get a taxi?	**Kur̃ galiù išsikviẽsti taksì?** [ˈkʊr gaˈlʲʊ ɪʃsʲɪkˈvʲɛstʲɪ takˈsʲɪ?]
Would you call a taxi for me, please?	**Ar̃ galė́tumėte mán iškviẽsti taksì?** [ar gaˈlʲeːtʊmʲeːte ˈman iʃkˈvʲɛstʲɪ takˈsʲɪ?]

Restaurant

Can I look at the menu, please?	**Ar̃ galiù gáuti meniù?** [ar ga'lʲʊ 'gɑʊtʲɪ mʲɛ'nʲʊ?]
Table for one.	**Stãlą vienám.** ['sta:lʲa: vʲiɛ'nam.]
There are two (three, four) of us.	**Mū̃sų dù (trỹs, keturì).** ['mu:su: 'dʊ ('tryi:s, ketʊ'rʲɪ).]

Smoking	**Rū̃kantiems** ['ru:kantʲiɛms]
No smoking	**Nerū̃kantiems** [nʲɛ'ru:kantʲiɛms]
Excuse me! (addressing a waiter)	**Atsiprašaũ!** [atsʲɪpra'ʃɑʊ!]
menu	**meniù** [mʲɛ'nʲʊ]
wine list	**vỹno meniù** ['vʲi:nɔ mʲɛ'nʲʊ]
The menu, please.	**Meniù, prašaũ.** [mʲɛ'nʲʊ, pra'ʃɑʊ.]

Are you ready to order?	**Ar̃ jaũ norésite užsisakýti?** [ar jɛʊ no'rʲe:sʲɪte ʊʒsʲɪsa'kʲi:tʲɪ?]
What will you have?	**Ką̃ užsisakýsite?** [ka: ʊʒsʲɪsa'kʲi:sʲɪtʲɛ?]
I'll have ...	**Àš paim̃siu ...** ['aʃ 'pʌɪmsʲʊ ...]

I'm a vegetarian.	**Àš vegetãras /vegetãrė/.** ['aʃ vege'ta:ras /vege'ta:rʲe:/.]
meat	**mėsõs** [mʲe:'so:s]
fish	**žuviẽs** [ʒʊ'vʲɛs]
vegetables	**daržóvės** [dar'ʒovʲe:s]

Do you have vegetarian dishes?	**Ar̃ tùrite vegetãriškų patiekalų̃?** [ar 'tʊrʲɪtʲɛ vʲɛgʲɛ'ta:rʲɪʃku: patʲiɛka'lʲʊ:?]
I don't eat pork.	**Àš neválgau kiaulíenos.** ['aʃ nʲɛ'valʲgɑʊ kʲɛʊ'lʲiɛnos.]
He /she/ doesn't eat meat.	**Jìs /jì/ neválgo mėsõs.** [jɪs /jɪ/ ne'valʲgɔ mʲe:'so:s.]
I am allergic to ...	**Àš alèrgiškas /alèrgiška/ ...** ['aʃ a'lʲɛrgʲɪʃkas /a'lʲɛrgʲɪʃka/ ...]

Would you please bring me ...	**Prašau atnešti man ...**
	[pra'ʃɑu at'nʲɛʃtʲɪ 'man ...]
salt | pepper | sugar	**druskos | pipirų | cukraus**
	['drʊskɔs | pʲɪ'pʲɪru: | 'tsʊkrɑus]
coffee | tea | dessert	**kavos | arbatos | desertą**
	[ka'vo:s | ar'ba:tos | dʲɛ'sʲɛrta:]
water | sparkling | plain	**vandeñs | gazuoto | negazuoto**
	[van'dʲɛns | ga'zuotɔ | nʲɛga'zuotɔ]
a spoon | fork | knife	**šaukštą | šakutę | peilį**
	['ʃɑukʃta: | ʃa'kʊtʲɛ: | 'pʲɛɪʲɪ:]
a plate | napkin	**lėkštę | servetėlę**
	[lʲe:kʃtʲɛ: | serve'tʲe:lʲɛ:]

Enjoy your meal!	**Skanaus!**
	[ska'nɑus!]
One more, please.	**Prašau dar vieną.**
	[pra'ʃɑu 'dar 'vʲɛna:.]
It was very delicious.	**Buvo labai skanu.**
	['bʊvɔ 'lʲa:bʌɪ ska'nʊ.]

check | change | tip	**sąskaita | grąža | arbatpinigiai**
	['sa:skʌɪta | gra:'ʒa | ar'ba:tpʲɪnʲɪgʲɛɪ]
Check, please.	**Sąskaitą, prašau.**
(Could I have the check, please?)	['sa:skʌɪta:, pra'ʃɑu.]
Can I pay by credit card?	**Ar galiu moketi kredito kortelė?**
	[ar ga'lʲʊ mo'kʲe:tʲɪ kre'dʲɪtɔ korte'lʲɛ?]
I'm sorry, there's a mistake here.	**Atsiprašau, bet jūs suklydote.**
	[atsʲɪpra'ʃɑu, bʲɛt 'ju:s sʊk'lʲi:dotʲɛ.]

Shopping

Can I help you?	**Kuõ galiù padéti?** ['kʋɑ ga'lʲʋ pa'dʲe:tʲɪ?]
Do you have ...?	**Ar̃ tùrite ...?** [ar 'tʋrʲɪtʲɛ ...?]
I'm looking for ...	**Íeškau ...** ['ɪɛʃkaʋ ...]
I need ...	**Mán reĩkia ...** ['man 'rʲɛɪkʲɛ ...]
I'm just looking.	**Àš tìk apžiūrinéju.** ['aʃ tʲɪk apʒʲu:rʲɪ'nʲe:jʋ.]
We're just looking.	**Mẽs tìk apžiūrinéjame.** ['mʲæs 'tʲɪk apʒʲu:rʲɪ'nʲe:jame.]
I'll come back later.	**Sugrĩšiu véliaũ.** [sʋg'rʲɪːʃʋ vʲe:'lʲɛʋ.]
We'll come back later.	**Sugrĩšime véliaũ.** [sʋg'rʲɪːʃɪme vʲe:'lʲɛʋ.]
discounts | sale	**núolaidos | išpardavìmas** ['nʋolʲʌɪdos | iʃparda'vʲɪmas]
Would you please show me ...	**Paródykite mán, prašaũ, ...** [pa'rodʲi:kʲɪtʲɛ 'man, pra'ʃɑʋ, ...]
Would you please give me ...	**Dúokite mán, prašaũ, ...** ['dʋokʲɪtʲɛ 'man, pra'ʃɑʋ, ...]
Can I try it on?	**Ar̃ galiù pasimatúoti?** [ar ga'lʲʋ pasʲɪma'tʋotʲɪ?]
Excuse me, where's the fitting room?	**Atsiprašaũ, kur̃ yrà matãvimosi kabìnos?** [atsʲɪpra'ʃɑʋ, kʋr i:'ra ma'ta:vʲɪmosʲɪ ka'bʲɪnos?]
Which color would you like?	**Kokiõs spalvõs norétumėte?** [kɔ'kʲɔ:s spalʲʲvo:s no'rʲe:tʋmʲe:te?]
size | length	**dỹdis | ìlgis** ['dʲi:dʲɪs | 'iˑlʲgʲɪs]
How does it fit?	**Ar̃ tiñka?** [ar 'tʲɪŋka?]
How much is it?	**Kíek taĩ kainúoja?** ['kʲiɛk 'tʌɪ kʌɪ'nʋo:jɛ?]
That's too expensive.	**Per̃ brangù.** ['pʲɛr bran'gʋ.]
I'll take it.	**Paim̃siu.** ['pʌɪmsʲʋ.]

Excuse me, where do I pay?

Atsiprašaũ, kur̃ galiu sumokéti?
[atsʲɪpraˈʃɑʊ, kʊr gaˈlʲʊ sʊmoˈkʲeːtʲɪ?]

Will you pay in cash or credit card?

Mokésite grynaĩs ar̃ kredìto kortelè?
[moˈkʲeːsʲɪte grʲiːˈnʌɪs ar krʲɛˈdʲɪtɔ korteˈlʲɛ?]

In cash | with credit card

grynaĩs | kredìto kortelè
[grʲiːˈnʌɪs | krʲɛˈdʲɪtɔ kortʲɛˈlʲɛ]

Do you want the receipt?

Ar̃ reĩkia čèkio?
[ar ˈrʲɛɪkʲɛ ˈtʂʲɛkʲɔ?]

Yes, please.

Taĩp.
[ˈtʌɪp.]

No, it's OK.

Nè, nereĩkia.
[ˈnʲɛ, nʲɛˈrʲɛɪkʲæ.]

Thank you. Have a nice day!

Ãčiū. Vìso gẽro.
[ˈaːtʂʲuː. ˈvʲɪsɔ ˈgʲærɔ.]

In town

Excuse me, please.	**Atsiprašaū, ...** [atsʲɪpraˈʃɑʊ.]
I'm looking for ...	**Íeškau ...** [ˈrʲɛʃkɑʊ ...]

the subway	**metrò** [mʲɛˈtro]
my hotel	**sàvo viẽšbučio** [ˈsavɔ ˈvʲɛʃbʊtʂʲɔ]
the movie theater	**kìno teãtro** [ˈkʲɪnɔ tʲɛˈɑːtrɔ]
a taxi stand	**taksì stotẽlę** [takˈsʲɪ stoˈtʲælʲɛː]

an ATM	**bankomãto** [baŋkoˈmaːtɔ]
a foreign exchange office	**valiùtos keitỹklos** [vaˈlʲʊtos kʲɛɪˈtʲiːklos]
an internet café	**internèto kavìnės** [ɪnterˈnʲɛtɔ kavʲɪˈnʲeːs]
... street	**... gãtvės** [... gaːtʲvʲeːs]
this place	**šiõs viẽtos** [ˈʃoːs ˈvʲɛtos]

Do you know where ... is?	**Ar̃ žìnote, kur̃ yrà ...?** [ar ˈʒʲɪnotʲɛ, kʊr iːˈra ...?]
Which street is this?	**Kokià čià gãtvė?** [kɔˈkʲæ tʂʲæ ˈgaːtvʲeː?]

Show me where we are right now.	**Paródykite, kur̃ dabar̃ ẽsame.** [paˈrodʲiːkʲɪtʲɛ, kʊr daˈbar ˈɛsamʲɛ.]
Can I get there on foot?	**Ar̃ galiù nueĩti teñ pėsčiomìs?** [ar gaˈlʲʊ ˈnʊɛɪtʲɪ ten pʲeːstʂʲoˈmʲɪs?]
Do you have a map of the city?	**Ar̃ tùrite miẽsto žemélapį?** [ar ˈtʊrʲɪtʲɛ ˈmʲɪːɛstɔ ʒɛˈmʲeːlʲapʲɪː?]

How much is a ticket to get in?	**Kíek kainúoja įėjìmo bìlietas?** [ˈkʲiɛk kʌɪˈnʊɑːjɛ iːɛˈjɪmɔ ˈbʲɪlʲiɛtas?]
Can I take pictures here?	**Ar̃ čià galimà fotografúoti?** [ar ˈtʂʲæ galʲɪˈma fotograˈfʊotʲɪ?]
Are you open?	**Ar̃ jū̃s veĩkiate?** [ar ˈjuːs ˈvʲɛɪkʲætʲɛ?]

When do you open?

Kadà atsidãrote?
[ka'da atsʲɪ'da:rotʲɛ?]

When do you close?

Kadà užsidãrote?
[ka'da ʊʒsʲɪ'da:rotʲɛ?]

Money

money	**pinigai** [pʲɪnʲɪ'gʌɪ]
cash	**grynieji** [grʲi:'nʲiɛjɪ]
paper money	**banknotai** [baŋk'notʌɪ]
loose change	**monetos** [mo'nʲɛtos]
check | change | tip	**sąskaita | grąžą | arbatpinigiai** ['sa:skʌɪta | gra:'ʒa | ar'ba:tpʲɪnʲɪgʲɛɪ]

credit card	**kredito kortelė** [krʲɛ'dʲɪtɔ kor'tʲælʲe:]
wallet	**piniginė** [pʲɪnʲɪ'gʲɪnʲe:]
to buy	**pirkti** ['pʲɪrktʲɪ]
to pay	**mokėti** [mo'kʲe:tʲɪ]
fine	**bauda** [bɑʊ'da]
free	**nemokamai** [nʲɛ'mokamʌɪ]

Where can I buy ...?	**Kur galiu nusipirkti ...?** ['kʊr ga'lʲʊ nʊsʲɪ'pʲɪrktʲɪ ...?]
Is the bank open now?	**Ar bankas jau dirba?** [ar 'baŋkas 'jɛʊ 'dʲɪrba?]
When does it open?	**Kada atsidaro?** [ka'da atsʲɪ'da:ro?]
When does it close?	**Kada užsidaro?** [ka'da ʊʒsʲɪ'da:ro?]

How much?	**Kiek?** ['kʲiɛk?]
How much is this?	**Kiek tai kainuoja?** ['kʲiɛk 'tʌɪ kʌɪ'nʊo:jɛ?]
That's too expensive.	**Per brangu.** ['pʲɛr bran'gʊ.]

Excuse me, where do I pay?	**Atsiprašau, kur galiu sumokėti?** [atsʲɪpra'ʃɑʊ, kʊr ga'lʲʊ sʊmo'kʲe:tʲɪ?]
Check, please.	**Čekį, prašau.** ['tʂʲɛkʲɪː, pra'ʃɑʊ.]

Can I pay by credit card?

Ar galiù mokéti kredìto kortelè?
[ar ga'lʲʊ mo'kʲeːtʲɪ kre'dʲɪtɔ korte'lʲɛ?]

Is there an ATM here?

Ar čià yrà bankomãtas?
[ar 'tʂʲæ iː'ra baŋko'maːtas?]

I'm looking for an ATM.

Ìeškau bankomãto.
['rʲɛʃkɑʊ baŋko'maːtɔ.]

I'm looking for a foreign exchange office.

Ìeškau valiùtos keitỹklos.
['rʲɛʃkɑʊ va'lʲʊtos kʲɛɪ'tʲiːklos.]

I'd like to change ...

Nóriu pasikeìsti ...
['norʲʊ pasʲɪ'kʲɛɪstʲɪ ...]

What is the exchange rate?

Kóks valiùtos kùrsas?
['koks va'lʲʊtos 'kʊrsas?]

Do you need my passport?

Ar reìkia màno pãso?
[ar 'rʲɛɪkʲɛ 'manɔ 'paːsɔ?]

Time

What time is it?	**Kíek dabar̃ valandų̃?** ['kʲiɛk da'bar val'an'du:?]
When?	**Kadà?** [ka'da?]
At what time?	**Kadà?** [ka'da?]
now | later | after ...	**dabar̃ | vėliaũ | põ ...** [da'bar | vʲe:'lʲɛu | 'po: ...]
one o'clock	**pìrmą vãlandą** ['pʲɪrma: 'va:lʲanda:]
one fifteen	**põ pirmõs penkiólika** ['po: pʲɪr'mo:s pʲɛŋ'kʲolʲɪka]
one thirty	**pùsė dviejų̃** ['pusʲe: dvʲiɛ'ju:]
one forty-five	**bė penkiólikos dvì** ['bʲɛ pʲɛŋ'kʲolʲɪkos dvʲɪ]
one | two | three	**pirmà | antrà | trečià** [pʲɪr'ma | an'tra | trʲɛ'tʂʲæ]
four | five | six	**ketvirtà | penktà | šeštà** [kʲɛtvʲɪr'ta | pʲɛŋk'ta | ʃɛʃ'ta]
seven | eight | nine	**septintà | aštuntà | devintà** [sʲɛptʲɪn'ta | aʃtʊn'ta | dʲɛvʲɪn'ta]
ten | eleven | twelve	**dešimtà | vienúolikta | dvýlikta** [dʲɛʃɪm'ta | vʲiɛ'nʊolʲɪkta | 'dvʲi:lʲɪkta]
in ...	**ùž ...** ['ʊʒ ...]
five minutes	**penkiũ minùčių** [pʲɛŋ'kʲu: mʲɪ'nʊtʂʲu:]
ten minutes	**dešimt minùčių** ['dʲæʃɪmt mʲɪ'nʊtʂʲu:]
fifteen minutes	**penkiólikos minùčių** [pʲɛŋ'kʲolʲɪkos mʲɪ'nʊtʂʲu:]
twenty minutes	**dvìdešimt minùčių** ['dvʲɪdʲɛʃɪmt mʲɪ'nʊtʂʲu:]
half an hour	**pùsvalandžio** ['pusvalʲandʒʲɔ]
an hour	**valandõs** [valʲan'do:s]

in the morning	**rytè** [ri:'tɛ]
early in the morning	**ankstì rytè** [aŋk'stɪ ri:'tɛ]
this morning	**šįryt** ['ʃɪ:rɪ:t]
tomorrow morning	**rýt rytè** ['ri:t ri:'tɛ]

in the middle of the day	**per̃ pietùs** ['pɛr piɛ'tʊs]
in the afternoon	**põ pietų̃** ['po: piɛ'tu:]
in the evening	**vakarè** [vaka'rɛ]
tonight	**šią̃nakt** ['ʃæ:nakt]

at night	**nãktį** ['na:kti:]
yesterday	**vãkar** ['va:kar]
today	**šiañdien** ['ʃændiɛn]
tomorrow	**rytój** [ri:'toj]
the day after tomorrow	**porýt** [po'ri:t]

What day is it today?	**Kokià šiañdien dienà?** [kɔ'kæ 'ʃændiɛn diɛ'na?]
It's ...	**Šiañdien yrà ...** ['ʃændiɛn i:'ra ...]
Monday	**pirmãdienis** [pɪr'ma:diɛnɪs]
Tuesday	**antrãdienis** [an'tra:diɛnɪs]
Wednesday	**trečiãdienis** [triɛ'tʂædiɛnɪs]

Thursday	**ketvirtãdienis** [kɛtvɪr'ta:diɛnɪs]
Friday	**penktãdienis** [pɛŋk'ta:diɛnɪs]
Saturday	**šeštãdienis** [ʃɛʃ'ta:diɛnɪs]
Sunday	**sekmãdienis** [sɛk'ma:diɛnɪs]

Greetings. Introductions

Hello.
Sveikì.
[svʲɛɪ'kʲɪ.]

Pleased to meet you.
Malonù susipažìnti.
[malʲo'nʊ sʊsʲɪpa'ʒʲɪntʲɪ.]

Me too.
Mán ìrgi.
['man 'irgʲɪ.]

I'd like you to meet ...
Nóriu, kàd susipažìntum sù ...
['norʲʊ, 'kad sʊsʲɪpa'ʒʲɪntʊm 'sʊ ...]

Nice to meet you.
Malonù susipažìnti.
[malʲo'nʊ sʊsʲɪpa'ʒʲɪntʲɪ.]

How are you?
Kaìp laìkotės?
['kʌɪp 'lʲʌɪkotʲeːs?]

My name is ...
Mãno va͂rdas ...
['maːnɔ vardas ...]

His name is ...
Jõ va͂rdas ...
[jɔː 'vardas ...]

Her name is ...
Jì vardù ...
['jɪ var'dʊ ...]

What's your name?
Kuõ jū̃s vardù?
['kʊɑ 'juːs var'dʊ?]

What's his name?
Kuõ jìs vardù?
['kʊɑ jɪs var'dʊ?]

What's her name?
Kuõ jì vardù?
['kʊɑ jɪ var'dʊ?]

What's your last name?
Kokià jū̃sų pavardė̃?
[kɔ'kʲæ 'juːsuː pavar'dʲeː?]

You can call me ...
Gãli manè vadìnti ...
['gaːlʲɪ ma'nʲɛ va'dʲɪntʲɪ ...]

Where are you from?
Ìš kur̃ jū̃s ẽsate?
[ɪʃ 'kʊr 'juːs 'ɛsatʲɛ?]

I'm from ...
Àš ìš ...
['aʃ ɪʃ ...]

What do you do for a living?
Kuõ užsìimate?
['kʊɑ ʊʒ'sʲɪimatʲɛ?]

Who is this?
Kàs tàs žmogùs?
['kas 'tas ʒmo'gʊs?]

Who is he?
Kàs jìs?
['kas 'jɪs?]

Who is she?
Kàs jì?
['kas jɪ?]

Who are they?	**Kàs jiẽ?**
	['kas jɪɛ?]
This is ...	**Taĩ ...**
	['tʌɪ ...]
my friend (masc.)	**mãno draũgas**
	['ma:nɔ 'drɑʊgas]
my friend (fem.)	**mãno draugĕ**
	['ma:nɔ drɑʊ'gʲe:]
my husband	**mãno výras**
	['ma:nɔ 'vʲi:ras]
my wife	**mãno žmonà**
	['ma:nɔ ʒmo'na]

my father	**màno tévas**
	['manɔ 'tʲe:vas]
my mother	**mãno mamà**
	['ma:nɔ ma'ma]
my brother	**mãno brólis**
	['ma:nɔ 'brolʲɪs]
my sister	**mãno sesuõ**
	['ma:nɔ sʲɛ'sʊɑ]
my son	**mãno sūnùs**
	['ma:nɔ su:'nʊs]
my daughter	**mãno dukrà**
	['ma:nɔ dʊk'ra]

This is our son.	**Taĩ mū́sų sūnùs.**
	['tʌɪ 'mu:su: su:'nʊs.]
This is our daughter.	**Taĩ mū́sų dukrà.**
	['tʌɪ 'mu:su: dʊk'ra.]
These are my children.	**Taĩ mãno vaikaĩ.**
	['tʌɪ 'ma:nɔ vʌɪ'kʌɪ.]
These are our children.	**Taĩ mū́sų vaikaĩ.**
	['tʌɪ 'mu:su: vʌɪ'kʌɪ.]

Farewells

Good bye!	**Vìso gẽro!** ['vʲɪsɔ 'gʲæro!]
Bye! (inform.)	**Ikì!** [ɪ'kʲɪ!]
See you tomorrow.	**Pasimatýsim rýt.** [pasʲɪma'tʲiːsʲɪm 'rʲiːt.]
See you soon.	**Greĩtai pasimatýsime.** ['grʲɛɪtʌɪ pasʲɪma'tʲiːsʲɪmʲɛ.]
See you at seven.	**Pasimatýsime septiñtą.** [pasʲɪma'tʲiːsʲɪmʲɛ sʲɛp'tʲɪnta:.]
Have fun!	**Pasilìnksminkite!** [pasʲɪ'lʲɪŋksmʲɪŋkʲɪtʲɛ!]
Talk to you later.	**Pašnekésim vẽliaũ.** [paʃnʲɛ'kʲeːsʲɪm vʲeː'lʲɛʊ.]
Have a nice weekend.	**Gẽro savaĩtgalio.** ['gʲæro sa'vʌɪtgalʲɔ.]
Good night.	**Labãnakt.** [lʲa'baːnakt.]
It's time for me to go.	**Mán jaũ laĩkas eĩti.** ['man 'jɛʊ 'lʲʌɪkas 'ɛɪtʲɪ.]
I have to go.	**Mán reĩkia eĩti.** ['man 'rʲɛɪkʲɛ 'ɛɪtʲɪ.]
I will be right back.	**Tuõj grĩšiu.** ['tʊɑj 'grʲɪːʃʊ.]
It's late.	**Jaũ vẽlù.** ['jɛʊ vʲeː'lʲʊ.]
I have to get up early.	**Mán reĩkia ankstì kéltis.** ['man 'rʲɛɪkʲɛ aŋk'stʲɪ 'kʲɛlʲtʲɪs.]
I'm leaving tomorrow.	**Àš išvykstù rýt.** ['aʃ iʃvʲiːksʲtʊ 'rʲiːt.]
We're leaving tomorrow.	**Mẽs išvýkstame rýt.** ['mʲæs iʃ'vʲiːkstamʲɛ 'rʲiːt.]
Have a nice trip!	**Gẽros keliõnės!** [gʲæros kʲɛ'lʲoːnʲeːs!]
It was nice meeting you.	**Bùvo malonù susipažìnti.** ['bʊvɔ malʲo'nʊ sʊsʲɪpa'ʒʲɪntʲɪ.]
It was nice talking to you.	**Bùvo malonù pasišnekéti.** ['bʊvɔ malʲo'nʊ pasʲɪʃnʲɛ'kʲeːtʲɪ.]
Thanks for everything.	**Ãčiū ùž vìską.** ['aːtʃʲu: 'ʊʒ 'vʲɪska:.]

I had a very good time.

Puĩkiai praléidau laĩką.
[pʊɪkʲɛɪ praˈlʲɛɪdɑʊ ˈlʌɪkaː.]

We had a very good time.

Mẽs puĩkiai praléidome laĩką.
[ˈmʲæs ˈpʊɪkʲɛɪ praˈlʲɛɪdomʲɛ ˈlʌɪkaː.]

It was really great.

Bùvo tikraĩ smagù.
[ˈbʊvɔ tʲɪkˈrʌɪ smaˈɡʊ.]

I'm going to miss you.

Pasiĩlgsiu tavẽs.
[pasʲɪˈlʲɡsʲʊ taˈvʲɛːs.]

We're going to miss you.

Pasiĩlgsime júsų.
[pasʲɪˈlʲɡsʲɪmʲɛ ˈjuːsuː.]

Good luck!

Sėkmẽs!
[sʲeːkˈmʲeːs!]

Say hi to ...

Pérduokite linkéjimus ...
[ˈpʲɛrdʊakʲɪtʲɛ lʲɪŋˈkʲɛjɪmʊs ...]

Foreign language

I don't understand.	**Nesuprantu.** [nʲɛsʊpranˈtʊ.]
Write it down, please.	**Užrašykite, prašau.** [ʊʒraˈʃɪːkʲɪtʲɛ, praˈʃɑʊ.]
Do you speak ...?	**Ar kalbate ...?** [ar ˈkalʲbatʲɛ ...?]
I speak a little bit of ...	**Truputį kalbu ...** [trʊˈpʊti: kalʲˈbʊ ...]
English	**angliškai** [ˈanglʲɪʃkʌɪ]
Turkish	**turkiškai** [ˈtʊrkʲɪʃkʌɪ]
Arabic	**arabiškai** [aˈraːbʲɪʃkʌɪ]
French	**prancūziškai** [pranˈtsuːzʲɪʃkʌɪ]
German	**vokiškai** [ˈvokʲɪʃkʌɪ]
Italian	**itališkai** [ɪˈtaːlʲɪʃkʌɪ]
Spanish	**ispaniškai** [ɪsˈpaːnʲɪʃkʌɪ]
Portuguese	**portugališkai** [portʊˈgaːlʲɪʃkʌɪ]
Chinese	**kiniškai** [ˈkʲɪnʲɪʃkʌɪ]
Japanese	**japoniškai** [jaˈponʲɪʃkʌɪ]
Can you repeat that, please.	**Ar galite pakartoti?** [ar ˈgaːlʲɪtʲɛ pakarˈtotʲɪ?]
I understand.	**Suprantu.** [sʊpranˈtʊ.]
I don't understand.	**Nesuprantu.** [nʲɛsʊpranˈtʊ.]
Please speak more slowly.	**Ar galite kalbéti lėčiau?** [ar ˈgaːlʲɪtʲɛ kalʲˈbʲeːtʲɪ lʲeːˈtʃʲɛʊ?]
Is that correct? (Am I saying it right?)	**Ar teisingai?** [ar tʲɛɪˈsʲɪngʌɪ?]
What is this? (What does this mean?)	**Ką tai reiškia?** [ka: ˈtʌɪ ˈrʲɛɪʃkʲæ?]

Apologies

Excuse me, please.   **Atléiskite.**
[at'lɛɪskʲɪtʲɛ.]

I'm sorry.   **Atsiprašaũ.**
[atsʲɪpra'ʃɑʊ.]

I'm really sorry.   **Mán labaĩ gaĩla.**
['man lʲa'bʌɪ 'gʌɪlʲa.]

Sorry, it's my fault.   **Atsiprašaũ, taĩ aš káltas /kaltà/.**
[atsʲɪpra'ʃɑʊ, 'tʌɪ aʃ 'kalʲtas /kal'ta/.]

My mistake.   **Taĩ máno klaidà.**
['tʌɪ 'maːnɔ klʲʌɪ'da.]

May I ...?   **Ar̃ galiù ...?**
[ar ga'lʲʊ ...?]

Do you mind if I ...?   **Ar̃ jū̃s niẽko priẽš, jéi ...?**
[ar 'juːs 'nʲɛkɔ 'prʲɛʃ, jɛɪ ...?]

It's OK.   **Niẽko tókio.**
['nʲɛkɔ 'tokʲɔ.]

It's all right.   **Vìskas geraĩ.**
['vʲɪskas gʲɛ'rʌɪ.]

Don't worry about it.   **Nesijáudinkite dě̃l tõ.**
[nʲɛsʲɪ'jɑʊdʲɪŋkʲɪtʲe 'dʲeːlʲ 'toː.]

Agreement

Yes.   **Taip.**
                        ['tʌɪp.]

Yes, sure.   **Žinoma.**
                        ['ʒɪnoma.]

OK (Good!)   **Gerai.**
                        [gʲɛ'rʌɪ.]

Very well.   **Puiku.**
                        [puɪ'ku.]

Certainly!   **Būtinai!**
                        [buːtʲɪ'nʌɪ!]

I agree.   **Sutinku.**
                        [sutʲɪŋ'ku.]

That's correct.   **Tikrai.**
                        [tʲɪk'rʌɪ.]

That's right.   **Teisingai.**
                        [tʲɛɪ'sʲɪŋgʌɪ.]

You're right.   **Jūs teisus /teisi/.**
                        ['juːs tʲɛɪ'sus /tʲɛɪ'sʲɪ/.]

I don't mind.   **Man tinka.**
                        ['man 'tʲɪŋka.]

Absolutely right.   **Tikrai taip.**
                        [tʲɪk'rʌɪ 'tʌɪp.]

It's possible.   **Įmanoma.**
                        [iː'maːnoma.]

That's a good idea.   **Gera mintis.**
                        [gʲɛ'ra mʲɪn'tʲɪs.]

I can't say no.   **Negaliu atsisakyti.**
                        [nʲɛga'lʲu atsʲɪsa'kʲiːtʲɪ.]

I'd be happy to.   **Mielai.**
                        [mʲiɛ'lʲʌɪ.]

With pleasure.   **Su mielu noru.**
                        ['su 'mʲiɛlʲu 'noru.]

Refusal. Expressing doubt

No.
Nè.
['nʲɛ.]

Certainly not.
Tikraì nè.
[tʲɪk'rʌɪ nʲɛ.]

I don't agree.
Àš nesutinkù.
['aʃ nʲɛsʊtʲɪŋ'kʊ.]

I don't think so.
Nemanaũ.
[nʲɛma'nɑʊ.]

It's not true.
Taì netiesà.
['tʌɪ nʲɛtʲiɛ'sa.]

You are wrong.
Jũs klýstate.
['juːs 'klʲiːstatʲɛ.]

I think you are wrong.
Manaũ, jũs klýstate.
[ma'nɑʊ, 'juːs 'klʲiːstatʲɛ.]

I'm not sure.
Nesù tìkras /tikrà/.
[nʲɛ'sʊ 'tʲɪkras /tʲɪk'ra/.]

It's impossible.
Neįmãnoma.
[nʲɛɪ'maːnoma.]

Nothing of the kind (sort)!
Niẽko panašaũs!
['nʲɛkɔ pana'ʃɑʊs!]

The exact opposite.
Vìsiškai príešingai.
['vʲɪsʲɪʃkʌɪ 'prʲiɛʃɪŋgʌɪ.]

I'm against it.
Àš prieštaráuju.
['aʃ prʲiɛʃta'rɑʊjʊ.]

I don't care.
Mán nerũpi.
['man nʲɛ'ruːpʲɪ.]

I have no idea.
Neįsivaizdúoju.
[nʲɛɪsʲɪvʌɪz'dʊoːjʊ.]

I doubt it.
Abejóju.
[abʲɛ'jɔjʊ.]

Sorry, I can't.
Atsiprašaũ, bèt negaliù.
[atsʲɪpra'ʃɑʊ, bʲɛt nʲɛga'lʲʊ.]

Sorry, I don't want to.
Atsiprašaũ, bèt nenóriu.
[atsʲɪpra'ʃɑʊ, bʲɛt nʲɛ'nɔrʲʊ.]

Thank you, but I don't need this.
Áčiū, bèt mán nereĩkia.
['aːtʃʲuː, bʲɛt 'man nʲɛ'rʲɛɪkʲæ.]

It's getting late.
Jaũ vėlù.
['jɛʊ vʲeː'lʲʊ.]

I have to get up early.

Mán reĩkia ankstì kéltis.
['man 'rɛɪkʲɛ aŋk'stʲɪ 'kʲɛlʲtʲɪs.]

I don't feel well.

Nesijaučiù geraĩ.
[nʲɛsʲɪjɛʊ'tʃʲʊ gʲɛ'rʌɪ.]

Expressing gratitude

Thank you.	**Ãčiū.** ['a:tʂʲu:.]
Thank you very much.	**Labaĩ ãčiū.** [lʲa'bʌɪ 'a:tʂʲu:.]
I really appreciate it.	**Àš labaĩ dėkìngas /dėkìnga/.** ['aʃ lʲa'bʌɪ dʲe:'kʲɪngas /dʲe:'kʲɪnga/.]
I'm really grateful to you.	**Labaĩ jùms dėkóju.** [lʲa'bʌɪ 'jums dʲe:'ko:jʊ.]
We are really grateful to you.	**Mẽs jùms labaĩ dėkìngi.** ['mʲæs 'jums lʲa'bʌɪ dʲe:'kʲɪngʲɪ.]
Thank you for your time.	**Ãčiū už jūsų laĩką.** ['a:tʂʲu: 'ʊʒ 'ju:su: 'lʲʌɪka:.]
Thanks for everything.	**Ãčiū už vìską.** ['a:tʂʲu: 'ʊʒ 'vʲɪska:.]
Thank you for ...	**Ãčiū už ...** ['a:tʂʲu: 'ʊʒ ...]
your help	**pagálbą** [pa'galʲba:]
a nice time	**smagiaĩ praléistą laĩką** [sma'gʲɛɪ pra'lʲɛɪsta: 'lʌɪka:]
a wonderful meal	**nuostãbų pãtiekalą** [nʊɑ'sta:bu: 'pa:tʲiɛkalʲa:]
a pleasant evening	**malõnų vãkarą** [ma'lʲo:nu: 'va:kara:]
a wonderful day	**nuostãbią diẽną** [nʊɑ'sta:bʲæ: 'dʲɛna:]
an amazing journey	**nuostãbią keliõnę** [nʊɑ'sta:bʲæ: kʲɛ'lʲo:nʲɛ:]
Don't mention it.	**Nėrà už ką̃.** [nʲe:'ra 'ʊʒ ka:.]
You are welcome.	**Nedėkókite.** [nʲɛdʲe:'kokʲɪte.]
Any time.	**Bèt kadà.** ['bʲɛt ka'da.]
My pleasure.	**Bùvo malonù padéti.** ['bʊvɔ malʲo'nʊ pa'dʲe:tʲɪ.]
Forget it.	**Ką̃ jūs, vìskas geraĩ.** [ka: 'ju:s, 'vʲɪskas gʲɛ'rʌɪ.]
Don't worry about it.	**Nesijáudinkite dėl tõ.** [nʲɛsʲɪ'jɑʊdʲɪŋkʲɪte 'dʲe:lʲ 'to:.]

Congratulations. Best wishes

Congratulations!	**Sveikinu!** ['svʲɛɪkʲɪnʊ!]
Happy birthday!	**Sù gimìmo dienà!** ['sʊ gʲɪ'mʲɪmɔ dʲɪɛ'na!]
Merry Christmas!	**Linksmų̃ Kalė̃dų!** [lʲɪŋks'mu: ka'lʲeːdu:!]
Happy New Year!	**Sù Naujaĩsiais mẽtais!** ['sʊ nɑʊ'jʌɪsʲɛɪs 'mʲætʌɪs!]

Happy Easter!	**Sù Šventõm Velýkom!** ['sʊ ʃvʲɛn'tom vʲɛ'lʲiːkom!]
Happy Hanukkah!	**Sù Chanùka!** ['sʊ xa'nʊka!]

I'd like to propose a toast.	**Nóriu paskélbti tõstą.** ['norʲʊ pas'kʲɛlʲptʲɪ 'tosta:.]
Cheers!	**Į̃ sveikãtą!** [iː svʲɛɪ'kaːta:!]
Let's drink to …!	**Išgérkime ùž …!** [ɪʃ'gʲɛrkʲɪmʲɛ 'ʊʒ …!]
To our success!	**Ùž mū́sų sėkmę̃!** ['ʊʒ 'muːsu: 'sʲeːkmʲɛ:!]
To your success!	**Ùž jū́sų sėkmę̃!** ['ʊʒ 'juːsu: 'sʲeːkmʲɛ:!]

Good luck!	**Sėkmė̃s!** [sʲeːk'mʲeːs!]
Have a nice day!	**Gẽros diẽnos!** ['gʲɛros 'dʲɛnos!]
Have a good holiday!	**Gerų̃ atóstogų!** [gʲɛ'ru: a'tostogu:!]
Have a safe journey!	**Saũgios keliõnės!** ['sɑʊgʲos ke'lʲoːnʲeːs!]
I hope you get better soon!	**Lìnkiu greĩtai pasveĩkti!** ['lʲɪŋkʲʊ 'grʲɛɪtʌɪ pas'vʲɛɪktʲɪ!]

Socializing

Why are you sad?	**Kodėl tau liūdna?** [ko'dʲeːl 'tɒʊ ˡluːd'na?]
Smile! Cheer up!	**Nusišypsok! Pralinksmėk!** [nʊsˡɪʃɪːp'sok! pralʲɪŋk'smʲeːk!]
Are you free tonight?	**Ar jūs šiandien neužsiėmę?** [ar ˈjuːs ˈʃændʲiɛn neʊʒ'sʲɪeːmʲɛ:?]
May I offer you a drink?	**Ar galiu tau pasiūlyti išgerti?** [ar ga'lʲʊ 'tɒʊ pa'sʲuːlʲiːtʲɪ iʃ'gʲɛrtʲɪ?]
Would you like to dance?	**Ar norėtum pašokti?** [ar no'rʲeːtʊm pa'ʃoktʲɪ?]
Let's go to the movies.	**Gal eikime į kiną?** ['galʲ 'ɛɪkʲɪmʲɛ iː 'kʲɪːna:?]
May I invite you to …?	**Ar galiu tave pakviesti …?** [ar ga'lʲʊ ta'vʲɛ pak'vʲɛstʲɪ …?]
a restaurant	**į restoraną** [iː rʲɛsto'raːna:]
the movies	**į kiną** [iː 'kʲɪːna:]
the theater	**į teatrą** [iː tʲɛ'aːtra:]
go for a walk	**pasivaikščioti** [pasʲɪ'vʌɪkʃtʃʲotʲɪ]
At what time?	**Kada?** [ka'da?]
tonight	**šiąnakt** ['ʃæːnakt]
at six	**šeštą** ['ʃæʃta:]
at seven	**septintą** [sʲɛp'tʲɪnta:]
at eight	**aštuntą** [aʃ'tʊnta:]
at nine	**devintą** [dʲɛ'vʲɪnta:]
Do you like it here?	**Ar tau čia patinka?** [ar 'tɒʊ tʂʲæ pa'tʲɪŋka?]
Are you here with someone?	**Ar tu ne viena?** [ar 'tʊ nʲɛ 'vʲiɛna?]
I'm with my friend.	**Aš su draugu /draugė/.** ['aʃ 'sʊ drɒʊ'gʊ /drɒʊ'gʲɛ/.]

I'm with my friends.	**Àš sù draugaìs /draugėmìs/.** ['aʃ 'sʊ drɑʊ'gʌɪs /drɑʊgʲe:'mʲɪs/.]
No, I'm alone.	**Nè, àš víena.** ['nʲɛ, aʃ 'vʲiɛna.]

Do you have a boyfriend?	**Ar̃ tùri vaikìną?** [ar 'tʊrʲɪ vʌɪ'kʲɪna:?]
I have a boyfriend.	**Turiù vaikìną.** [tʊ'rʲʊ vʌɪ'kʲɪna:.]
Do you have a girlfriend?	**Ar̃ tùri mergìną?** [ar 'tʊrʲɪ mʲɛr'gʲɪna:?]
I have a girlfriend.	**Turiù mergìną.** [tʊ'rʲʊ mʲɛr'gʲɪna:.]

Can I see you again?	**Ar̃ gãlime dár kadà pasimatýti?** [ar 'ga:lʲɪmʲɛ 'dar ka'da pasʲɪma'tʲi:tʲɪ?]
Can I call you?	**Ar̃ galiù táu paskam̃binti?** [ar ga'lʲʊ 'tɑʊ pas'kambʲɪntʲɪ?]
Call me. (Give me a call.)	**Paskam̃bink mán.** [pas'kambʲɪŋk 'man.]
What's your number?	**Kóks tàvo nùmeris?** ['koks 'tavɔ 'nʊmʲɛrʲɪs?]
I miss you.	**Pasiìlgau tavę̃s.** [pasʲɪ'ɪlʲgɑʊ ta'vʲɛ:s.]

You have a beautiful name.	**Tàvo gražùs var̃das.** ['tavɔ gra'ʒʊs 'vardas.]
I love you.	**Mýliu tavè.** ['mʲi:lʲʊ ta'vʲɛ.]
Will you marry me?	**Ar̃ tekési ùž manę̃s?** [ar te'kʲe:sʲɪ 'ʊʒ ma'nʲɛ:s?]
You're kidding!	**Tù juokáuji!** ['tʊ jʊɑ'kɑʊjɪ!]
I'm just kidding.	**Àš juokáuju.** ['aʃ jʊɑ'kɑʊjʊ.]

Are you serious?	**Ar̃ tù rimtaĩ?** [ar 'tʊ rʲɪm'tʌɪ?]
I'm serious.	**Àš rimtaĩ.** ['aʃ rʲɪm'tʌɪ.]
Really?!	**Tikraĩ?** [tʲɪk'rʌɪ?]
It's unbelievable!	**Neĩtikétina!** [nʲɛɪ:tʲɪ'kʲe:tʲɪna!]
I don't believe you.	**Nètikiu.** ['nʲɛtʲɪkʲʊ.]
I can't.	**Àš negaliù.** ['aʃ nʲɛga'lʲʊ.]
I don't know.	**Nežinaũ.** [nʲɛʒʲɪ'nɑʊ.]
I don't understand you.	**Nesuprantù tavę̃s.** [nʲɛsʊpran'tʊ ta'vʲɛ:s.]

Please go away.	**Prašaū atstók.** [praˈʃɔʊ atsˈtok.]
Leave me alone!	**Palìk manè víeną!** [paˈlʲɪk maˈnʲɛ ˈvʲiɛnaː!]

I can't stand him.	**Àš negaliù jõ pakę̃st.** [ˈaʃ nʲɛgaˈlʲʊ jɔː paˈkʲɛːst.]
You are disgusting!	**Tù šlykštùs!** [ˈtʊ ʃlʲiːkʃˈtʊs!]
I'll call the police!	**Àš iškvíesiu polìciją!** [ˈaʃ iʃkˈvʲɛsʲʊ poˈlʲɪtsʲɪja:!]

Sharing impressions. Emotions

I like it.	**Mán patiñka.** ['man pa'tʲɪŋka.]
Very nice.	**Labaĩ gražù.** [lʲa'bʌɪ gra'ʒʊ.]
That's great!	**Puikù!** [pʊi'kʊ!]
It's not bad.	**Neblogaĩ.** [nʲɛblʲo'gʌɪ.]

I don't like it.	**Mán nepatiñka.** ['man nʲɛpa'tʲɪŋka.]
It's not good.	**Taĩ nérà geraĩ.** ['tʌɪ nʲeː'ra ge'rʌɪ.]
It's bad.	**Taĩ blogaĩ.** ['tʌɪ blʲogʌɪ.]
It's very bad.	**Taĩ labaĩ blogaĩ.** ['tʌɪ lʲa'bʌɪ blʲo'gʌɪ.]
It's disgusting.	**Taĩ šlykštù.** [tʌɪ ʃlʲiːkʃ'tʊ.]

I'm happy.	**Àš laimìngas /laimìnga/.** ['aʃ lʲʌɪ'mʲɪngas /lʲʌɪ'mʲɪnga/.]
I'm content.	**Àš paténkintas /paténkinta/.** ['aʃ pa'tʲɛŋkʲɪntas /patʲɛŋkʲɪnta/.]
I'm in love.	**Àš įsimyléjes /įsimyléjusi/.** ['aʃ iːsʲɪmʲɪː'lʲe:jɛ:s /iːsʲɪmʲɪː'lʲe:jʊsʲɪ/.]
I'm calm.	**Àš ramùs /ramì/.** ['aʃ ra'mʊs /ra'mʲɪ/.]
I'm bored.	**Mán nuobodù.** ['man nʊɑbo'dʊ.]

I'm tired.	**Àš pavar̃ges /pavar̃gusi/.** ['aʃ pa'vargʲɛ:s /pa'vargʊsʲɪ/.]
I'm sad.	**Mán liũdnà.** ['man 'lʲu:d'na.]
I'm frightened.	**Àš išsigañdes /išsigañdusi/.** ['aʃ iʃsʲɪ'gandʲɛ:s /iʃsʲɪ'gandʊsʲɪ/.]
I'm angry.	**Àš supýkes /supýkusi/.** ['aʃ sʊ'pʲiːkʲɛ:s /sʊ'pʲiːkʊsʲɪ/.]

I'm worried.	**Àš susirū́pines /susirū́pinusi/.** ['aʃ sʊsʲɪ'ru:pʲɪnʲɛ:s /sʊsʲɪ'ru:pʲɪnʊsʲɪ/.]
I'm nervous.	**Àš susinèrvines /susinèrvinusi/.** ['aʃ sʊsʲɪ'nʲɛrvʲɪnʲɛ:s /sʊsʲɪ'nʲɛrvʲɪnʊsʲɪ/.]

I'm jealous. (envious)

Àš pavýdžiu.
['aʃ pa'vʲiːdʒʲʊ.]

I'm surprised.

Àš nustẽbęs /nustẽbusi/.
['aʃ nʊstʲæbʲɛːs /nʊstʲæbʊsʲɪ/.]

I'm perplexed.

Àš sumìšęs /sumìšusi/.
['aʃ sʊ'mʲɪʃɛːs /sʊ'mʲɪʃʊsʲɪ/.]

Problems. Accidents

I've got a problem.
Atsitìko problemà.
[atsʲɪ'tʲɪkɔ problʲɛ'ma.]

We've got a problem.
Mẽs tùrime problemà.
['mʲæs 'turʲɪmʲɛ problʲɛ'ma.]

I'm lost.
Àš pasiklýdau.
['aʃ pasʲɪk'lʲiːdɑʊ.]

I missed the last bus (train).
Nespėjau į̃ paskutìnį autobùsą (traukinį).
[nʲɛs'pʲeːʲjɛʊ iː pasku'tʲɪːnʲɪ ɑʊto'busa: ('trɑʊkʲɪnʲɪː).]

I don't have any money left.
Nebeturiù pinigų̃.
[nʲɛbʲɛtʊ'rʲʊ pʲɪnʲɪ'guː.]

I've lost my ...
Àš pàmečiau ...
['aʃ 'pamʲɛtʲʂʲɛʊ ...]

Someone stole my ...
Kažkàs pàvogė màno ...
[kaʒ'kas 'pavogʲeː 'manɔ ...]

passport
pãsą
['paːsa:]

wallet
pinigìnę
[pʲɪnʲɪ'gʲɪnʲɛː]

papers
dokumentùs
[dokʊmʲɛn'tʊs]

ticket
bìlietą
['bʲɪlʲiɛta:]

money
pìnigus
['pʲɪnʲɪgʊs]

handbag
rañkinę
['raŋkʲɪnʲɛː]

camera
fotoaparãtą
[fotoapa'ra:ta:]

laptop
nešiojamąjį kompiùterį
[nʲɛ'ʃojama:jiː kom'pʲʊtʲɛrʲɪː]

tablet computer
planšètinį kompiùterį
[plʲan'ʃɛtʲɪnʲɪː kom'pʲʊtʲɛrʲiː]

mobile phone
mobìlųjį telefòną
[mo'bʲɪluːjiː tʲɛlʲɛ'fona:]

Help me!
Padékite mán!
[pa'dʲeːkʲɪte 'man!]

What's happened?
Kàs atsitìko?
['kas atsʲɪ'tʲɪko?]

fire	**gaĩsras** [ˈgʌɪsras]
shooting	**kažkàs šáudė** [kaʒˈkas ˈʃɑʊdʲe:]
murder	**žmogžudỹstė** [ʒmogʒʊˈdʲi:stʲe:]
explosion	**sprogìmas** [sproˈgʲɪmas]
fight	**muštỹnės** [mʊʃˈtʲi:nʲe:s]

Call the police!	**Kvíeskite polìciją!** [ˈkvʲɛskʲɪtʲɛ poˈlʲɪtsʲɪja:!]
Please hurry up!	**Prašaũ, paskubékite!** [praˈʃɑʊ, paskʊˈbʲeːkʲɪtʲe!]
I'm looking for the police station.	**Íeškau polìcijos skýriaus.** [ˈɪɛʃkɑʊ poˈlʲɪtsɪjos ˈskʲiːrʲɛʊs.]
I need to make a call.	**Mán reĩkia paskambìnti.** [ˈman ˈrʲɛɪkʲɛ pasˈkambʲɪntʲɪ.]
May I use your phone?	**Aȓ galiù pasinaudóti jū́sų telefonù?** [ar gaˈlʲʊ pasʲɪnɑʊˈdotʲɪ ˈjuːsu: tʲɛlʲɛfoˈnʊ?]

I've been ...	**Manè ...** [maˈnʲɛ ...]
mugged	**apipléšė** [apʲɪˈplʲeːʃe:]
robbed	**àpvogė** [ˈapvogʲe:]
raped	**išprievartãvo** [ɪʃprʲɪɛvarˈtaːvɔ]
attacked (beaten up)	**užpúolė** [ʊʒˈpʊolʲe:]

Are you all right?	**Aȓ vìskas geraĩ?** [ar ˈvʲɪskas gʲɛˈrʌɪ?]
Did you see who it was?	**Aȓ mãtėte, kàs taĩ bùvo?** [ar ˈmaːtʲete, ˈkas tʌɪ ˈbʊvo?]
Would you be able to recognize the person?	**Aȓ sugebétumėte atpažìnti tą̃ žmõgų?** [ar sʊgeˈbʲeːtʊmʲete atpaˈʒʲɪntʲɪ ta: ˈʒmogu:?]
Are you sure?	**Aȓ jū̃s tìkras /tikrà/?** [ar ˈjuːs tʲɪkras /tʲɪkˈra/?]

Please calm down.	**Prašaũ, nurìmkite.** [praˈʃɑʊ, nʊˈrʲɪmkʲɪtʲɛ.]
Take it easy!	**Ramiaũ!** [raˈmʲɛʊ!]
Don't worry!	**Nesijáudinkite!** [nʲɛsʲɪˈjɑʊdʲɪŋkʲɪtʲɛ!]
Everything will be fine.	**Vìskas bùs geraĩ.** [ˈvʲɪskas ˈbʊs gʲɛˈrʌɪ.]

Everything's all right.

Vìskas geraĩ.
['vʲɪskas gʲɛ'rʌɪ.]

Come here, please.

Prašaũ, ateĩkite čià.
[pra'ʃɑʊ, a'tʲɛɪkʲɪtʲɛ tʂʲæ.]

I have some questions for you.

Turiù jùms kẽletą kláusimų.
[tʊ'rʲʊ 'jʊms 'kʲælʲɛta: 'klɑʊsʲɪmu:.]

Wait a moment, please.

Prašaũ trupùtį paláukti.
[pra'ʃɑʊ trʊ'pʊtʲɪ: pa'lʲɑʊktʲɪ.]

Do you have any I.D.?

Aȓ tùrite kokiùs nórs asmeñs dokumentùs?
[ar 'tʊrʲɪtʲɛ ko'kʲʊs 'nors as'mʲɛns dokʊmʲɛn'tʊs?]

Thanks. You can leave now.

Ãčiū. Gãlite eĩti.
['a:tʂʲu:. 'ga:lʲɪtʲɛ 'ɛɪtʲɪ.]

Hands behind your head!

Rankàs ùž galvõs!
[raŋ'kas 'ʊʒ galʲvo:s!]

You're under arrest!

Jū̃s sùimamas!
['ju:s 'sʊimamas!]

Health problems

Please help me.	**Prašaũ, padékite mán.** [pra'ʃɑʊ, padʲeːkʲɪte 'man.]
I don't feel well.	**Mán blogà.** ['man blʲoˈga.]
My husband doesn't feel well.	**Mãno výrui blogà.** ['maːnɔ 'vʲiːrʊɪ blʲoˈga.]
My son ...	**Mãno sũnui ...** ['manɔ 'suːnʊɪ ...]
My father ...	**Mãno tévui ...** ['manɔ 'tʲeːvʊɪ ...]
My wife doesn't feel well.	**Mãno žmónai blogà.** ['manɔ 'ʒmonʌɪ blʲoˈga.]
My daughter ...	**Mãno dùkrai ...** ['manɔ 'dʊkrʌɪ ...]
My mother ...	**Mãno mãmai ...** ['manɔ 'maːmʌɪ ...]
I've got a ...	**Mán ...** ['man ...]
headache	**skaũda gálvą** ['skɑʊda 'galʲva:]
sore throat	**skaũda gérklę** ['skɑʊda 'gʲɛrklʲɛ:]
stomach ache	**skaũda skrañdį** ['skɑʊda 'skrandʲɪ:]
toothache	**skaũda dañtį** ['skɑʊda 'danti:]
I feel dizzy.	**Mán svaĩgsta galvà.** ['man 'svʌɪgsta galʲva.]
He has a fever.	**Jìs karščiúoja.** [jɪs karʃ'tsʲʊoːjɛ.]
She has a fever.	**Jì karščiúoja.** [jɪ karʃ'tsʲʊoːjɛ.]
I can't breathe.	**Negaliù kvépúoti.** [nʲɛga'lʲʊ kvʲeːˈpʊotʲɪ.]
I'm short of breath.	**Mán sunkù kvépúoti.** ['man sʊŋ'kʊ kvʲeːˈpʊotʲɪ.]
I am asthmatic.	**Sergù astmà.** [sʲɛrˈgʊ ast'ma.]
I am diabetic.	**Sergù diabetù.** [sʲɛrˈgʊ dʲæbʲɛ'tʊ.]

I can't sleep.	**Negaliu užmigti.** [nʲɛga'lʲʊ ʊʒ'mʲɪktʲɪ.]
food poisoning	**apsinuõdijimas maistù** [apsʲɪ'nʊɑdʲɪjimas mʌɪs'tʊ]

It hurts here.	**Skaũda čia.** ['skɑʊda 'tsʲæ.]
Help me!	**Padékite mán!** [pa'dʲeːkʲɪte 'man!]
I am here!	**Àš čia!** ['aʃ tsʲæ!]
We are here!	**Mẽs čia!** ['mʲæs tsʲæ!]
Get me out of here!	**Ištráukite manè ìš čia!** [ɪʃ'trɑʊkʲɪtʲɛ ma'nʲɛ ɪʃ tsʲæ!]
I need a doctor.	**Mán reĩkia dãktaro.** ['man 'rʲɛɪkʲɛ 'daːktarɔ.]
I can't move.	**Negaliu pajudéti.** [nʲɛga'lʲʊ pajʊ'dʲeːtʲɪ.]
I can't move my legs.	**Negaliu pajùdinti kójų.** [nʲɛga'lʲʊ pa'jʊdʲɪntʲɪ 'koju:.]

I have a wound.	**Àš sùžeistas /sùžeistà/.** ['aʃ 'sʊʒʲɛɪstas /sʊʒʲɛɪs'ta/.]
Is it serious?	**Aȓ žaizdà sunkì?** [ar ʒʌɪz'da sʊŋ'kʲɪ?]
My documents are in my pocket.	**Mãno dokumeñtai kišẽnéje.** ['maːnɔ dokʊ'mentʌɪ kʲɪʃʲænʲeːje.]
Calm down!	**Nurìmkite!** [nʊrʲɪmkʲɪtʲɛ!]
May I use your phone?	**Aȓ galiù pasinaudóti jũsų telefonù?** [ar ga'lʲʊ pasʲɪnɑʊ'dotʲɪ 'ju:su: tʲɛlʲɛfo'nʊ?]

Call an ambulance!	**Kviẽskite greĩtąją!** ['kvʲɛskʲɪtʲɛ 'grʲɛɪtaːja:!]
It's urgent!	**Taĩ skubù!** ['tʌɪ skʊ'bʊ!]
It's an emergency!	**Taĩ skubùs ãtvejis!** ['tʌɪ skʊ'bʊs 'a:tvʲɛjis!]
Please hurry up!	**Prašaũ, paskubékite!** [pra'ʃɑʊ, paskʊ'bʲeːkʲɪte!]
Would you like please call a doctor?	**Aȓ gãlite iškviẽsti dãktarą?** [ar 'gaːlʲɪtʲɛ iʃk'vʲɛstʲɪ 'daːktara:?]
Where is the hospital?	**Kuȓ ligóninė?** ['kʊr lʲɪ'gonʲɪnʲeː?]

How are you feeling?	**Kaĩp jaũčiatės?** ['kʌɪp 'jɛʊtsʲætʲeːs?]
Are you all right?	**Aȓ vìskas geraĩ?** [ar 'vʲɪskas gʲɛ'rʌɪ?]
What's happened?	**Kàs atsitìko?** ['kas atsʲɪ'tʲɪko?]

I feel better now.

Jaučiúosi geriaũ.
[jɛʊ'tʂʲʊosʲɪ gʲɛ'rʲɛʊ.]

It's OK.

Vìskas tvarkojė.
['vʲɪskas tvarko'jæ.]

It's all right.

Vìskas geraĩ.
['vʲɪskas gʲɛ'rʌɪ.]

At the pharmacy

pharmacy (drugstore)	**vaistinė** ['vʌɪstʲɪnʲeː]
24-hour pharmacy	**vìsą parą dìrbanti vaistinė** ['vʲɪsa: 'pa:ra: 'dʲɪrbantʲɪ 'vʌɪstʲɪnʲeː]
Where is the closest pharmacy?	**Kur yrà artimiáusia vaistinė?** ['kʊr iː'ra artʲɪ'mʲæʊsʲɛ 'vʌɪstʲɪnʲeː?]

Is it open now?	**Ar jì dabar̃ dìrba?** [ar jɪ da'bar 'dʲɪrba?]
At what time does it open?	**Kadà jì atsidãro?** [ka'da jɪ atsʲɪ'da:ro?]
At what time does it close?	**Kadà jì užsidãro?** [ka'da jɪ ʊʒsʲɪ'da:ro?]

Is it far?	**Ar jì tóli?** [ar jɪ 'toːlʲɪ?]
Can I get there on foot?	**Ar galiù nueĩti teñ pésčiomìs?** [ar ga'lʲʊ 'nʊʲɛɪtʲɪ ten pʲeːstsʲo'mʲɪs?]
Can you show me on the map?	**Ar gãlite paródyti žemélapyje?** [ar 'ga:lʲɪte pa'rodʲiːtʲɪ ʒeˈmʲeːlapʲiːje?]

Please give me something for ...	**Dúokite mán kažką̃ nuõ ...** ['dʊokʲɪtʲɛ 'man kaʒ'ka: nʊɑ ...]
a headache	**galvõs skaũsmo** [galʲ'voːs 'skɑʊsmɔ]
a cough	**kosùlio** [kɔ'sʊlʲɔ]
a cold	**péršalimo** ['pʲɛrʃalʲɪmɔ]
the flu	**grìpo** ['grʲɪpɔ]

a fever	**karščiãvimo** [karʃ'tsʲævʲɪmɔ]
a stomach ache	**skrañdžio skaũsmo** ['skrandʒʲɔ 'skɑʊsmɔ]
nausea	**pỹkinimo** ['pʲiːkʲɪnʲɪmɔ]
diarrhea	**viduriãvimo** [vʲɪdʊ'rʲævʲɪmɔ]
constipation	**vidurių̃ užkietéjimo** [vʲɪdʊ'rʲuː ʊʒkʲɪɛ'tʲɛjɪmɔ]
pain in the back	**nùgaros skaũsmo** ['nʊgaros 'skɑʊsmɔ]

chest pain	**krutinės skausmo** [krʊtʲɪˈnʲeːs ˈskɑʊsmɔ]
side stitch	**šóno diegimo** [ˈʃonɔ dʲiɛˈgʲɪmɔ]
abdominal pain	**pilvo skausmo** [ˈpʲɪlʲvɔ ˈskɑʊsmɔ]

pill	**tabletė** [tabˈlʲɛtʲeː]
ointment, cream	**tepalas, krèmas** [ˈtʲæpalʲas, ˈkrʲɛmas]
syrup	**sirupas** [ˈsʲɪrʊpas]
spray	**purškalas** [ˈpʊrʃkalʲas]
drops	**lašai** [lʲaˈʃʌɪ]

You need to go to the hospital.	**Jùms reikia į ligóninę.** [ˈjʊms ˈrʲɛɪkʲɛ iː lʲɪˈgonʲɪnʲɛː]
health insurance	**sveikatos draudimas** [svʲɛɪˈkaːtos drɑʊˈdʲɪmas]
prescription	**vaisto receptas** [ˈvʌɪstɔ rʲɛˈtsʲɛptas]
insect repellant	**vabzdžių repeleñtas** [vabzˈdʒʲuː rʲɛpʲɛˈlʲɛntas]
Band Aid	**pleistras** [ˈplʲɛɪstras]

The bare minimum

Excuse me, ...
Atsiprašaŭ, ...
[atsʲɪpra'ʃɑʊ, ...]

Hello.
Sveiki.
[svʲɛɪ'kʲɪ.]

Thank you.
Áčiū.
['a:tʂʲu:.]

Good bye.
Iki.
[ɪ'kʲɪ.]

Yes.
Taip.
['tʌɪp.]

No.
Nè.
['nʲɛ.]

I don't know.
Nežinaŭ.
[nʲɛʒɪ'nɑʊ.]

Where? | Where to? | When?
Kur̃? | Kur? | Kadà?
['kʊr? | 'kʊr? | ka'da?]

I need ...
Mán reĩkia ...
['man 'rʲɛɪkʲɛ ...]

I want ...
Nóriu ...
['norʲʊ ...]

Do you have ...?
Ar̃ tùrite ...?
[ar 'tʊrʲɪtʲɛ ...?]

Is there a ... here?
Ar̃ čià yrà ...?
[ar 'tʂʲæ i:'ra ...?]

May I ...?
Ar̃ galiù ...?
[ar ga'lʲʊ ...?]

..., please (polite request)
Prašaŭ ...
[pra'ʃɑʊ ...]

I'm looking for ...
Íeškau ...
['ɪʲɛʃkɑʊ ...]

restroom
tualèto
[tʊa'lʲɛtɔ]

ATM
bankomãto
[baŋko'ma:tɔ]

pharmacy (drugstore)
vaistinės
['vʌɪstʲɪnʲe:s]

hospital
ligóninės
[lʲɪ'gonʲɪnʲe:s]

police station
polìcijos skỹriaus
[po'lʲɪtsɪjɔs 'skʲi:rʲɛʊs]

subway
metrò
[mʲɛ'tro]

taxi	**taksì** [tak'sʲɪ]
train station	**traukinių stotiẽs** [trɑʊkʲɪ'nʲu: sto'tʲɛs]

My name is ...	**Mãno vaȓdas ...** ['ma:nɔ 'vardas ...]
What's your name?	**Kuõ jũs vardù?** ['kʊɑ 'ju:s var'dʊ?]
Could you please help me?	**Atsiprašaũ, aȓ gãlite padéti?** [atsʲɪpra'ʃɑʊ, ar 'ga:lʲɪte pa'dʲe:tʲɪ?]
I've got a problem.	**Atsitìko problemà.** [atsʲɪ't'ɪkɔ problʲɛ'ma.]
I don't feel well.	**Mán blogà.** ['man blʲo'ga.]
Call an ambulance!	**Kviẽskite greĩtąją!** ['kvʲɛskʲɪtʲɛ 'grʲɛɪta:ja:!]
May I make a call?	**Aȓ galiù paskambìnti?** [ar ga'lʲʊ pas'kambʲɪntʲɪ?]

I'm sorry.	**Atsiprašaũ.** [atsʲɪpra'ʃɑʊ.]
You're welcome.	**Nėrà ùž ką̃.** [nʲe:'ra 'ʊʒ ka:.]

I, me	**àš** ['aʃ]
you (inform.)	**tù** ['tʊ]
he	**jìs** [jɪs]
she	**jì** [jɪ]
they (masc.)	**jiẽ** ['jiɛ]
they (fem.)	**jõs** ['jɔ:s]
we	**mẽs** ['mʲæs]
you (pl)	**jũs** ['ju:s]
you (sg, form.)	**Jũs** ['ju:s]

ENTRANCE	**ĮÉJÌMAS** [i:ˈɛːˈjɪmas]
EXIT	**IŠÉJÌMAS** [ɪʃˈeːˈjɪmas]
OUT OF ORDER	**NEVEĨKIA** [nʲɛ'vʲɛɪkʲɛ]
CLOSED	**UŽDARÝTA** [ʊʒda'rʲi:ta]

OPEN

ATIDARYTA
[atɪda'riːta]

FOR WOMEN

MÓTERŲ
['motʲɛruː]

FOR MEN

VYRŲ
['vʲiːruː]

T&P BOOKS

MINI DICTIONARY

This section contains 250
useful words required for
everyday communication.
You will find the names of
months and days of the week
here. The dictionary also
contains topics such as colors,
measurements, family, and
more

T&P Books Publishing

DICTIONARY CONTENTS

T&P Books Publishing

time	**laĩkas** (v)	['lʲʌɪkas]
hour	**valandà** (m)	[valʲan'da]
half an hour	**pùsvalandis** (v)	['pʊsvalʲandʲɪs]
minute	**minùtė** (m)	[mʲɪ'nʊtʲe:]
second	**sekùndė** (m)	[sʲɛ'kʊndʲe:]
today (adv)	**šiañdien**	['ʃændʲiɛn]
tomorrow (adv)	**rytój**	[rʲi:'toj]
yesterday (adv)	**vãkar**	['va:kar]
Monday	**pirmãdienis** (v)	[pʲɪr'ma:dʲiɛnʲɪs]
Tuesday	**antrãdienis** (v)	[an'tra:dʲiɛnʲɪs]
Wednesday	**trečiãdienis** (v)	[trʲɛ'tʃʲædʲiɛnʲɪs]
Thursday	**ketvirtãdienis** (v)	[kʲɛtvʲɪr'ta:dʲiɛnʲɪs]
Friday	**penktãdienis** (v)	[pʲɛŋk'ta:dʲiɛnʲɪs]
Saturday	**šeštãdienis** (v)	[ʃɛʃ'ta:dʲiɛnʲɪs]
Sunday	**sekmãdienis** (v)	[sʲɛk'ma:dʲiɛnʲɪs]
day	**dienà** (m)	[dʲiɛ'na]
working day	**dárbo dienà** (m)	['darbɔ dʲiɛ'na]
public holiday	**šveñtinė dienà** (m)	['ʃvʲentʲɪnʲe: dʲiɛ'na]
weekend	**saváitgalis** (v)	[sa'vʌɪtgalʲɪs]
week	**saváitė** (m)	[sa'vʌɪtʲe:]
last week (adv)	**pràeitą saváitę**	['praʲɛɪta: sa'vʌɪtʲɛ:]
next week (adv)	**ateĩnančią saváitę**	[a'tʲɛɪnantʃʲæ: sa'vʌɪtʲɛ:]
in the morning	**rytè**	[rʲi:'tʲɛ]
in the afternoon	**popiẽt**	[pɔ'pʲɛt]
in the evening	**vakarè**	[vaka'rʲɛ]
tonight (this evening)	**šiañdien vakarè**	['ʃændʲiɛn vaka'rʲɛ]
at night	**nãktį**	['na:kti:]
midnight	**vidùrnaktis** (v)	[vʲɪ'dʊrnaktʲɪs]
January	**saũsis** (v)	['sɑʊsʲɪs]
February	**vasãris** (v)	[va'sa:rʲɪs]
March	**kovàs** (v)	[kɔ'vas]
April	**balañdis** (v)	[ba'lʲandʲɪs]
May	**gegužė̃** (m)	[gʲɛgʊ'ʒʲe:]
June	**biržẽlis** (v)	[bʲɪr'ʒʲælʲɪs]
July	**líepa** (m)	['lʲiɛpa]
August	**rugpjũtis** (v)	[rʊg'pju:tʲɪs]

September	rugsėjis (v)	[rʊg'sʲɛjɪs]
October	spalis (v)	['spaːlʲɪs]
November	lapkritis (v)	['lʲaːpkrʲɪtʲɪs]
December	gruodis (v)	['grʊɑdʲɪs]

in spring	pavasarį	[paˈvaːsarʲɪː]
in summer	vasarą	['vaːsaraː]
in fall	rudenį	['rʊdʲɛnʲɪː]
in winter	žiemą	['ʒʲɛmaː]

month	mėnuo (v)	['mʲeːnʊɑ]
season (summer, etc.)	sezonas (v)	[sʲɛ'zonas]
year	metai (v dgs)	['mʲætʌɪ]

2. Numbers. Numerals

0 zero	nulis	['nʊlʲɪs]
1 one	vienas	['vʲɛnas]
2 two	du	['dʊ]
3 three	tris	['trʲɪs]
4 four	keturi	[kʲɛtʊ'rʲɪ]

5 five	penki	[pʲɛŋ'kʲɪ]
6 six	šeši	[ʃɛ'ʃʲɪ]
7 seven	septyni	[sʲɛptʲiː'nʲɪ]
8 eight	aštuoni	[aʃtʊɑ'nʲɪ]
9 nine	devyni	[dʲɛvʲiː'nʲɪ]
10 ten	dešimt	['dʲæʃɪmt]

11 eleven	vienuolika	[vʲɛ'nʊɑlʲɪka]
12 twelve	dvylika	['dvʲiːlʲɪka]
13 thirteen	trylika	['trʲiːlʲɪka]
14 fourteen	keturiolika	[kʲɛtʊ'rʲɑlʲɪka]
15 fifteen	penkiolika	[pʲɛŋ'kʲɑlʲɪka]

16 sixteen	šešiolika	[ʃɛ'ʃɑlʲɪka]
17 seventeen	septyniolika	[sʲɛptʲiː'nʲɑlʲɪka]
18 eighteen	aštuoniolika	[aʃtʊɑ'nʲɑlʲɪka]
19 nineteen	devyniolika	[dʲɛvʲiː'nʲɑlʲɪka]

20 twenty	dvidešimt	['dvʲɪdʲɛʃɪmt]
30 thirty	trisdešimt	['trʲɪsdʲɛʃɪmt]
40 forty	keturiasdešimt	['kʲɛtʊrʲæsdʲɛʃɪmt]
50 fifty	penkiasdešimt	['pʲɛŋkʲæsdʲɛʃɪmt]

60 sixty	šešiasdešimt	['ʃæʃæsdʲɛʃɪmt]
70 seventy	septyniasdešimt	[sʲɛp'tʲiːnʲæsdʲɛʃɪmt]
80 eighty	aštuoniasdešimt	[aʃ'tʊɑnʲæsdʲɛʃɪmt]
90 ninety	devyniasdešimt	[dʲɛ'vʲiːnʲæsdʲɛʃɪmt]
100 one hundred	šimtas	['ʃɪmtas]

200 two hundred	dù šimtaĩ	['dʊ ʃɪm'tʌɪ]
300 three hundred	trìs šimtaĩ	['trʲɪs ʃɪm'tʌɪ]
400 four hundred	keturì šimtaĩ	[kʲɛtʊ'rʲɪ ʃɪm'tʌɪ]
500 five hundred	penkì šimtaĩ	[pʲɛŋ'kʲɪ ʃɪm'tʌɪ]

600 six hundred	šešì šimtaĩ	[ʃɛ'ʃɪ ʃɪm'tʌɪ]
700 seven hundred	septynì šimtaĩ	[sʲɛptʲiː'nʲɪ 'ʃɪmtʌɪ]
800 eight hundred	aštuonì šimtaĩ	[aʃtʊɑ'nʲɪ ʃɪm'tʌɪ]
900 nine hundred	devynì šimtaĩ	[dʲɛvʲiː'nʲɪ ʃɪm'tʌɪ]
1000 one thousand	tū́kstantis	['tu:kstantʲɪs]

| 10000 ten thousand | dẽšimt tū́kstančių | ['dʲæʃɪmt 'tu:kstantʃʲu:] |
| one hundred thousand | šiм̃tas tū́kstančių | ['ʃɪmtas 'tu:kstantʃʲu:] |

| million | milijõnas (v) | [mʲɪlʲɪ'jo:nas] |
| billion | milijárdas (v) | [mʲɪlʲɪ'jardas] |

3. Humans. Family

man (adult male)	výras (v)	['vʲi:ras]
young man	jaunuõlis (v)	[jɛʊ'nʊɑlʲɪs]
woman	móteris (m)	['motʲɛrʲɪs]
girl (young woman)	panẽlė (m)	[pa'nʲælʲe:]
old man	sẽnis (v)	['sʲænʲɪs]
old woman	sẽnė (m)	['sʲænʲe:]

mother	mótina (m)	['motʲɪna]
father	tévas (v)	['tʲe:vas]
son	sūnùs (v)	[su:'nʊs]
daughter	dukrà, duktě (m)	[dʊk'ra], [dʊk'tʲe:]
brother	brólis (v)	['brolʲɪs]
sister	sesuõ (m)	[sʲɛ'sʊɑ]

parents	tévaĩ (v)	[tʲe:'vʌɪ]
child	vaĩkas (v)	['vʌɪkas]
children	vaikaĩ (v)	[vʌɪ'kʌɪ]
stepmother	pãmotė (m)	['pa:motʲe:]
stepfather	patévis (v)	[pa'tʲe:vʲɪs]

grandmother	senẽlė (m)	[sʲɛ'nʲælʲe:]
grandfather	senẽlis (v)	[sʲɛ'nʲælʲɪs]
grandson	anũkas (v)	[a'nu:kas]
granddaughter	anũkė (m)	[a'nu:kʲe:]
grandchildren	anũkai (v)	[a'nu:kʌɪ]

uncle	dẽdė (v)	['dʲe:dʲe:]
aunt	tetà (m)	[tʲɛ'ta]
nephew	sūnénas (v)	[su:'nʲe:nas]
niece	dukterė́čia (m)	[dʊkte'rʲe:tʃʲæ]
wife	žmonà (m)	[ʒmo'na]

husband	výras (v)	['vʲiːras]
married (masc.)	vēdęs	['vʲædʲɛːs]
married (fem.)	ištekėjusi	[ɪʃtʲɛˈkʲeːjʊsʲɪ]
widow	našlě (m)	[naʃˈlʲe:]
widower	našlỹs (v)	[naʃˈlʲiːs]

| name (first name) | vardas (v) | ['vardas] |
| surname (last name) | pavardě (m) | [pavarˈdʲe:] |

relative	giminaitis (v)	[gʲɪmʲɪˈnaɪtʲɪs]
friend (masc.)	draŭgas (v)	['draʊgas]
friendship	draugỹstė (m)	[draʊˈgʲiːstʲe:]

partner	pártneris (v)	['partnʲɛrʲɪs]
superior (n)	vĩršininkas (v)	['vʲɪrʃɪnʲɪŋkas]
colleague	kolegà (v)	[kɔlʲɛˈga]
neighbors	kaimýnai (v)	[kʌɪˈmʲiːnʌɪ]

4. Human body

body	kũnas (v)	['ku:nas]
heart	širdìs (m)	[ʃɪrˈdʲɪs]
blood	kraũjas (v)	['kraʊjas]
brain	smẽgenys (v dgs)	['smʲægʲɛnʲiːs]

bone	káulas (v)	['kaʊlʲas]
spine (backbone)	stùburas (v)	['stʊbʊras]
rib	šónkaulis (v)	['ʃonkaʊlʲɪs]
lungs	plaũčiai (v)	['plʲaʊtʂʲɛɪ]
skin	óda (m)	['oda]

head	galvà (m)	[galʲˈva]
face	veĩdas (v)	['vʲɛɪdas]
nose	nósis (m)	['nosʲɪs]
forehead	kaktà (m)	[kakˈta]
cheek	skrúostas (v)	['skrʊɑstas]

mouth	burnà (m)	[bʊrˈna]
tongue	liežùvis (v)	[lʲiɛˈʒʊvʲɪs]
tooth	dantìs (v)	[danˈtʲɪs]
lips	lũpos (m dgs)	['lʲu:pos]
chin	smãkras (v)	['sma:kras]

ear	ausìs (m)	[aʊˈsʲɪs]
neck	kãklas (v)	['ka:klʲas]
eye	akìs (m)	[aˈkʲɪs]
pupil	vyzdýs (v)	[vʲiːzˈdʲiːs]
eyebrow	añtakis (v)	['antakʲɪs]
eyelash	blakstíena (m)	[blʲakˈstʲiɛna]
hair	plaukaĩ (v dgs)	[plʲaʊˈkʌɪ]

hairstyle	šukuosena (m)	[ʃʊˈkʊɑsʲɛna]
mustache	ūsai (v dgs)	[ˈuːsʌɪ]
beard	barzda (m)	[barzˈda]
to have (a beard, etc.)	nešioti	[nʲɛˈʃotʲɪ]
bald (adj)	plikas	[ˈplʲɪkas]

hand	plaštaka (m)	[ˈplʲaːʃtaka]
arm	ranka (m)	[raŋˈka]
finger	pirštas (v)	[ˈpʲɪrʃtas]
nail	nagas (v)	[ˈnaːgas]
palm	delnas (v)	[ˈdʲɛlʲnas]

shoulder	petis (v)	[pʲɛˈtʲɪs]
leg	koja (m)	[ˈkoja]
knee	kelias (v)	[ˈkʲælʲæs]
heel	kulnas (v)	[ˈkʊlⁿnas]
back	nugara (m)	[ˈnʊgara]

5. Clothing. Personal accessories

clothes	apranga (m)	[apranˈga]
coat (overcoat)	paltas (v)	[ˈpalʲtas]
fur coat	kailiniai (v dgs)	[kʌɪlʲɪˈnʲɛɪ]
jacket (e.g., leather ~)	striukė (m)	[ˈstrʲʊkʲeː]
raincoat (trenchcoat, etc.)	apsiaustas (v)	[apˈsʲɛʊstas]

shirt (button shirt)	marškiniai (v dgs)	[marʃkʲɪˈnʲɛɪ]
pants	kelnės (m dgs)	[ˈkʲɛlʲnʲeːs]
suit jacket	švarkas (v)	[ˈʃvarkas]
suit	kostiumas (v)	[kɔsˈtʲʊmas]

dress (frock)	suknelė (m)	[sʊkˈnʲælʲeː]
skirt	sijonas (v)	[sʲɪˈjɔːnas]
T-shirt	futbolininko marškiniai (v)	[ˈfʊtbolʲɪnʲɪŋkɔ marʃkʲɪˈnʲɛɪ]

bathrobe	chalatas (v)	[xaˈlʲaːtas]
pajamas	pižama (m)	[pʲɪʒaˈma]
workwear	darbo drabužiai (v)	[ˈdarbɔ draˈbʊʒʲɛɪ]

underwear	baltiniai (v dgs)	[balʲtʲɪˈnʲɛɪ]
socks	kojinės (m dgs)	[ˈkoːjɪnʲeːs]
bra	liemenėlė (m)	[lʲiɛmeˈnʲeːlʲeː]
pantyhose	pėdkelnės (m dgs)	[ˈpʲeːdkʲɛlʲnʲeːs]
stockings (thigh highs)	kojinės (m dgs)	[ˈkoːjɪnʲeːs]
bathing suit	maudymosi kostiumėlis (v)	[ˈmɑʊdʲɪːmosʲɪ kostʲʊˈmʲeːlʲɪs]

hat	kepurė (m)	[kʲɛˈpʊrʲeː]
footwear	avalynė (m)	[ˈaːvalʲiːnʲeː]
boots (e.g., cowboy ~)	auliniai batai (v)	[ɑʊˈlʲɪnʲɛɪ ˈbatʌɪ]

heel	kulnas (v)	['kuɫⁿas]
shoestring	bãtraištis (v)	['ba:trʌɪʃtʲɪs]
shoe polish	ãvalynės krèmas (v)	['a:valʲi:nʲe:s 'krʲɛmas]

gloves	pĩrštinės (m dgs)	['pʲɪrʃtʲɪnʲe:s]
mittens	kùmštinės (m dgs)	['kumʃtʲɪnʲe:s]
scarf (muffler)	šãlikas (v)	['ʃa:lʲɪkas]
glasses (eyeglasses)	akiniaĩ (dgs)	[akʲɪ'nʲɛɪ]
umbrella	skėtis (v)	['skʲe:tʲɪs]

tie (necktie)	kaklãraištis (v)	[kak'lʲa:rʌɪʃtʲɪs]
handkerchief	nósinė (m)	['nosʲɪnʲe:]
comb	šùkos (m dgs)	['ʃukos]
hairbrush	plaukų̃ šepetỹs (v)	[plʲaʊ'ku: ʃɛpʲɛ'tʲi:s]

buckle	sagtìs (m)	[sak'tʲɪs]
belt	dìržas (v)	['dʲɪrʒas]
purse	rankinùkas (v)	[raŋkʲɪ'nʊkas]

6. House. Apartment

apartment	bùtas (v)	['bʊtas]
room	kambarỹs (v)	[kamba'rʲi:s]
bedroom	miegamãsis (v)	[mʲiɛga'masʲɪs]
dining room	valgomãsis (v)	[valʲgo'masʲɪs]

living room	svečių̃ kambarỹs (v)	[svʲɛ'tʃʲu: kamba'rʲi:s]
study (home office)	kabinètas (v)	[kabʲɪ'nʲɛtas]
entry room	príeškambaris (v)	['prʲiɛʃkambarʲɪs]
bathroom (room with a bath or shower)	voniõs kambarỹs (v)	[vo'nʲo:s kamba'rʲi:s]
half bath	tualètas (v)	[tʊa'lʲɛtas]

vacuum cleaner	dulkių siurblỹs (v)	['dulʲkʲu: sʲʊr'blʲi:s]
mop	plaušìnė šlúota (m)	[plʲaʊ'ʃɪnʲe: 'ʃlʲʊata]
dust cloth	skùduras (v)	['skʊdʊras]
short broom	šlúota (m)	['ʃlʲʊata]
dustpan	semtuvėlis (v)	[sʲɛmtʊvʲe:lʲɪs]

furniture	baĩdai (v)	['balʲdʌɪ]
table	stãlas (v)	['sta:lʲas]
chair	kėdė̃ (m)	[kʲe:'dʲe:]
armchair	fòtelis (v)	['fotʲɛlʲɪs]

mirror	veĩdrodis (v)	['vʲɛɪdrodʲɪs]
carpet	kìlimas (v)	['kʲɪlʲɪmas]
fireplace	židinỹs (v)	[ʒʲɪdʲɪ'nʲi:s]
drapes	užúolaidos (m dgs)	[ʊ'ʒʊalʲʌɪdos]
table lamp	stalìnė lémpa (m)	[sta'lʲɪnʲe: 'lʲɛmpa]
chandelier	sietýnas (v)	[sʲiɛ'tʲi:nas]

kitchen	virtuvė (m)	[vʲɪrˈtʊvʲeː]
gas stove (range)	dujinė (m)	[ˈdʊjinʲeː]
electric stove	elektrinė (m)	[ɛlʲɛkˈtrʲɪnʲeː]
microwave oven	mikrobangų krosnėlė (m)	[mʲɪkrobanˈgu: krosˈnʲælʲeː]
refrigerator	šaldytuvas (v)	[ʃalʲdʲiːˈtʊvas]
freezer	šaldymo kamera (m)	[ˈʃalʲdʲiːmɔ ˈkaːmʲɛra]
dishwasher	indų plovimo mašina (m)	[ˈɪndu: plʲoˈvʲɪmɔ maʃɪˈna]
faucet	čiaupas (v)	[ˈtʂʲæʊpas]
meat grinder	mėsmalė (m)	[ˈmʲeːsmalʲeː]
juicer	sulčiaspaudė (m)	[sʊlʲˈtʂʲæspɑʊdʲeː]
toaster	tosteris (v)	[ˈtostʲɛrʲɪs]
mixer	mikseris (v)	[ˈmʲɪksʲɛrʲɪs]
coffee machine	kavos aparatas (v)	[kaˈvoːs apaˈraːtas]
kettle	arbatinukas (v)	[arbatʲɪˈnʊkas]
teapot	arbatinis (v)	[arbaːˈtʲɪnʲɪs]
TV set	televizorius (v)	[tʲɛlʲɛˈvʲɪzorʲʊs]
VCR (video recorder)	video magnetofonas (v)	[vʲɪdʲɛɔ magnʲɛtoˈfonas]
iron (e.g., steam ~)	lygintuvas (v)	[lʲiːgʲɪnˈtʊvas]
telephone	telefonas (v)	[tʲɛlʲɛˈfonas]